YOU GOT IN!
NOW WHAT?

PRAISE FOR *YOU GOT IN! NOW WHAT?*

"People who obsess about getting into college can forget that another, more important challenge comes after: actually getting the good of your education, allowing it to create the maximum enlargement of your powers. Funny, practical, wise, and rife with life lessons from successful contemporaries, Jay Hamilton's book meets this need head-on. This is an essential companion for anyone asking, 'I'm in. Now what?'—and maybe even more, for parents wondering how to truly help."

Richard Brodhead, President Emeritus, Duke University

"So many important parts of life are squished together into a four-year college experience: mind-bending ideas, new skills, brushes with love, difficult trade-offs, finding your people, and the very real consequences of an unsupervised soft-serve ice cream machine in your dining hall. This book offers a wide array of powerful provocations for how to take advantage of that messy, lovely, all-too-brief time when your day job is to be a student, and your real job is to learn to be yourself."

Sarah Stein Greenberg, Executive Director, Stanford d.school, and author of *Creative Acts for Curious People: How to Think, Create, and Lead in Unconventional Ways*

"*You Got In! Now What?* is a gem. Toss out all those 'college success' volumes that tell you to take good notes, go to professors' office hours, and learn time management skills. Hamilton offers students far deeper and more enduring lessons about how to make the most of your college education. Wise, insightful, engaging, and accessible, this book will transform the way you approach your education and your life. Read it before you begin college and return to it repeatedly. You won't find a better guide to navigating college."

Louis E. Newman, former Dean of Academic Advising, Stanford University, and author of *Thinking Critically in College: The Essential Handbook for Student Success*

"This is exactly the book I wish I had when I started college! In short, snappy, well-referenced chapters, it provides poignant advice and memorable stories about how to get the most out of your college experience."

Tina Seelig, Executive Director, Knight-Hennessy Scholars, Stanford University, and author of *What I Wish I Knew When I Was 20: A Crash Course on Making Your Place in the World*

YOU GOT IN! NOW WHAT?

100 Insights into Finding Your Best Life in College

JAMES T. HAMILTON

**ILLUSTRATED BY
JIM TOOMEY**

Radius Book Group
New York

Radius Book Group
A division of Diversion Publishing Corp.
www.radiusbookgroup.com

For more information, email info@radiusbookgroup.com

The publisher does not have any control over and does not assume any responsibility for author or third-party websites or their content.

First Radius Book Group Edition: March 2025
Paperback ISBN: 978-1-63576-887-9
e-ISBN: 978-1-63576-892-3

Book design by Scribe Inc.
Cover and jacket design by Tom Lau

Printed in the United States of America
10 9 8 7 6 5 4 3 2 1

CONTENTS

THINKING

CHOOSING

CONNECTING

IDENTITY

CITIZENSHIP

HOW TO GO WRONG

INTRODUCTION

What would you do if you could not fail?

Answering that question involves creativity, optimism, a sense of purpose, and some self-knowledge. This mix of qualities can also help you get the most out of college. But if you're like many students, you'll spend years preparing for and months applying to college. Once you're in, you'll spend less time thinking about how to make the most of this opportunity.

You're in good company. As a professor, I've spent thousands of hours leading classroom discussions and an equal number of hours in academic committee meetings. I've won eight teaching awards at Harvard, Duke, and Stanford and earned many accolades for my research. Yet like many teachers, I often thought about the goals of a college education only twice a year: at the welcoming convocation for new students in the fall and at commencement celebrations in the spring.

That changed when Stanford administrators asked for proposals about undergraduate education during the university's long-range planning process. I suggested the school create a book of essays about college for admitted students to read in the summer before they arrive. Writing that proposal led me to think hard about the goals of a liberal arts education.

I discovered there are seven.

Signaling

Economist Michael Spence won a Nobel Prize for developing the idea that a degree is valuable because it shows a person has surmounted costly admission and sorting hurdles. The degree is a profitable signal not because of the education it reflects but because of the qualities associated with gaining admission and graduating.

1

Networking

Here the value of a liberal arts school derives from the set of people you go to school with—in terms of both what you learn from them and your future career associations with them.

Domain-Specific Knowledge

Part of what you learn in college relates to specific facts and theories that help you solve problems in a given domain such as engineering or economics.

Critical Thinking Skills

These are the different ways of reasoning and analysis that give you insights into how to recognize, define, and solve problems across many areas. Such skills are often at the center of broad distribution requirements at liberal arts schools.

Self-Knowledge and Moral Development

Part of a liberal arts education can help you reflect on your own personal goals and values. Questions include: What is the nature of a good life? How might you prioritize family, friends, work, and community? How should you live your life?

Citizenship

Living in a community involves decisions about collective action, public goods, and social justice. At the individual level, you face many choices about whether to free ride off the efforts of others or contribute time, thought, and resources to group decisions. Education helps shape identities and values relating to community and political engagement and can instill greater interest and involvement in public affairs.

Intrinsic Love of Learning

Many types of knowledge and answers are sought to help you make and change decisions and thus are valued for instrumental reasons. Some ideas and topics are pursued primarily as puzzles and valued intrinsically. The journey to reason and to discover answers is both a pathway and a destination, pursued simply for fun.

This book is designed to help you achieve these seven goals during your time in college. To gather lessons about navigating college and life, I generated a large reading list of books by Stanford alums, books about alums, speeches at convocations and graduations, essays from the student newspaper, vignettes from the school magazine, and research by professors. In an era of AI summarization, I adopted an older approach: close reading accompanied by sifting and analysis.

I chose to base the book on insights from a single university following the adage of "Write what you know." I've been a Stanford department chair, professor, spouse, and parent. As Vice Provost for Undergraduate Education, I work to connect students with transformative intellectual experiences, including the school's Civic, Liberal, and Global Education program for first-year students.

The result is one hundred lessons about navigating your education and what comes afterward. Each is accompanied by an explanation from the writings of alums or professors and an illustration by award-winning cartoonist Jim Toomey. They're sorted into eight sections: Meaning, Purpose, Thinking, Choosing, Connecting, Identity, Citizenship, and How to Go Wrong.

Why should you read this book? Decisions about what to study, how to spend time outside the classroom, and when to power down can feel overwhelming. Students often aim for perfection, neglect their friends and health, avoid challenging experiences, or follow a path of familiar expectations. Life hacks and shortcuts cause them to miss out on what makes college valuable and interesting. You go through college only once, although many others before you have pursued this journey. This book offers you an opportunity to learn from their experiences.

Imagine if you could learn how others have navigated these challenges. You could ask alums to look back on friendships and careers and provide advice. Studies from the social sciences using data from others' jobs and lives could offer insights into how you should approach your life.

You don't have to imagine that opportunity. That's the pay-off promised from reading this book. Now that you've gotten into college, the next step is to develop a strategy of how to find your best life there.

There are three ways to use this book to do that. You can read the lessons in each section and pause to think through how they apply to your own life. A reflection at the end of each segment is designed to help you pull together these insights. Later, you can dive back into a particular lesson as your experiences in college help you recognize the challenges discussed. You may even decide to reread sections after your first quarter, semester, or year, deriving new takeaways based on your time in college.

These lessons are designed to help you make decisions. College involves a series of choices—about time, meaning, friends, family, health, classes, majors, and careers. These lessons have already changed how I spend my time. When I read the question "What would you do if you could not fail?" the answer was clear—write a book that helps students get the most out of college. I hope these lessons have a similar effect on how you choose to navigate college and your life beyond!

MEANING

1

PURSUE AN EDUCATION, NOT JUST THE DEGREE.

You got in, and someday you'll graduate. Your degree is a ticket into higher-paying professions.

College graduates earn $1.2 million more over their lifetimes relative to high school graduates. Economist Michael Spence won a Nobel Prize for his theory that a college education pays off because it's a signal to future employers about your quality.

It's hard to predict who will be productive on the job, but getting a degree shows that you've passed rigorous admissions screenings and devoted the time and money necessary to graduate. In Spence's signaling model, even if you learn little in college, the degree is valuable as an investment to demonstrate you're a highly productive person.

Focusing on the credential leads some students to approach school as a transaction. Tests and papers are exchanged for credits, paying off in a line on your resume. But this misses the many ways college can change you as a person.

Classes can shift your interests and values. Dining hall conversations with friends generate new perspectives and lifelong connections. Extracurriculars spark insights, skills, and fun.

If you focus primarily on the degree, you'll miss the freedom and serendipity of college as an education. The good news is that you can choose both. If you're open and adventurous about ideas, people, and experiences, you get knowledge and a credential.

And memories and friendships, which are their own form of riches.

2

DON'T LIVE
ANOTHER'S SCRIPT.

"I'm very disappointed. I'm not sure you'll ever amount to anything."

That's what Carly Fiorina's father said when she announced that she was quitting law school after three months. Law was central to her father's career, first as a professor and then as a federal judge. When she graduated from college, Fiorina believed her family expected her to follow her father's path.

Several months of law school left her uninspired, sleepless, and racked with headaches. Deliverance came in the form of a Sunday-morning shower when she realized, "It's *my* life. I can do what I want."

Her parents were disappointed, but she was happy. She recalls, "At twenty-two, at that moment, it finally dawned on me that my life couldn't be about pleasing my parents." She took a job as a receptionist, discovering a love of business and people. Fiorina ended up as the CEO of Hewlett-Packard and ran for the Republican presidential nomination in 2016.

Sandra Day O'Connor had a different reaction to the law but a similar insistence on finding her own way. She went through undergrad and law school in six years. Rejecting her parents' attempts to set her up with a potential match from a wealthy family, she wrote to them, "It is my life. . . . I want to lead an interesting life—I want to study, practice law. . . . Please be tolerant of my ideas and simply because I want something different from you don't think it is wrong, or wrong for me."

O'Connor graduated in the top 10 percent of her law class but could not get a single interview for an associate position at a law firm. She persevered and years later became what she called the FWOTSC: the First Woman on the Supreme Court.

3

THE UNEXAMINED LIFE
IS NOT WORTH LIVING.

Taking this idea from Socrates to heart can have life-altering results.

When Sterling K. Brown took a first-year requirement focused on philosophy, he found guides. Twenty years after graduating, he listed his "Big Three": Socrates, Plato, and Lao Tzu. Socrates's emphasis on the examined life of meaning and self-awareness made a deep impact on him. Brown had come to college with a plan: "Major in Econ, go into business, or finance, make BANK . . . and take care of my family."

Yet he fell in love with acting. Describing this transformation, he said, "The desire to illuminate the human condition was always the thing that gave my life the greatest sense of purpose. . . . I had to let go of who I was, in order to become who I am." That willingness to let go of one plan and learn from experience led to a life in acting and critical acclaim for his work in *The People v. O. J. Simpson*, *This Is Us*, and *Black Panther*.

When Cory Booker became a Rhodes Scholar, he said, "I decided to make a bit of a Socratic quest of it. . . . I went to England with the idea that I would spend those two years studying and exploring my ideas, my values, my choices, my actions, myself."

The future senator read Gandhi's autobiography and became inspired by its subtitle, *The Story of My Experiments with Truth*. Booker resolved to alter his consumer choices to reflect his values. Research on how eating meat affects the body, our climate, and animals led him to try being a vegetarian. After several months on the diet, he felt "supercharged" and stayed with this approach.

Several decades later, he became a vegan—after a final splurge at IHOP, which included this breakfast: "pumpkin pancakes, two orders of eggs with extra cheese, stuffed French toast, and hash browns." Sometimes choosing a new direction in life starts with a look back at what you're leaving.

4
LIFE IS SHORT.

You're going to die. Knowing that is liberating.

That's the insight Steve Jobs emphasized in his famous commencement address. Since he was seventeen, Jobs said,

> I have looked in the mirror every morning and asked myself: "If today were the last day of my life, would I want to do what I am about to do today?" And whenever the answer has been "No" for too many days in a row, I know I need to change something.
>
> Remembering that I'll be dead soon is the most important tool I've ever encountered to help me make the big choices in life. Because almost everything—all external expectations, all pride, all fear of embarrassment or failure—these things just fall away in the face of death, leaving only what is truly important. Remembering that you are going to die is the best way I know to avoid the trap of thinking you have something to lose. You are already naked. There is no reason not to follow your heart.

Out for a morning run, then twenty-four-year-old Phil Knight had a similar epiphany:

> I had an aching sense that our time is short, shorter than we ever know, short as a morning run, and I wanted mine to be meaningful. And purposeful. And creative. And important. Above all ... different....
>
> I told myself: Let everyone else call your idea crazy ... just keep going.... Whatever comes, just don't stop. That's the precocious, prescient, urgent advice I managed to give myself, out of the blue, and somehow managed to take.

Steve Jobs cofounded Apple. Phil Knight cofounded Nike. For both, acknowledging the limits of a lifespan generated exploration and urgency. For you, a willingness to take risks can turn college into an adventure to embrace.

5
BALANCE ACTION
AND CONTEMPLATION.

What does balance look like?

When Jennifer Summit and Blakey Vermeule taught "A Life of Action or a Life of Contemplation: Debates in Western Literature and Philosophy," the texts were often classical or early modern, but the concerns were current. What should matter in charting your course, personal interests or financial returns? What's more important to pursue, productivity or meaning?

Society frames these choices as either/or. The course provided an alternative view that there is "a necessary, continued tension in the well-lived life, whether between action and contemplation, theory and practice, work and leisure, or society and solitude."

Paul Kalanithi's path shows what balance looks like.

He approached college excited about taking classes in literature and biology, saying, "I felt less like someone preparing to climb a career ladder than a buzzing electron about to achieve escape velocity, flinging out into a strange and sparkling universe."

Kalanithi explored the life of the mind through reading T. S. Eliot, Nabokov, and Conrad. Neuroscience courses offered a framework for how the mind worked.

He noted, "Throughout college, my monastic, scholarly study of human meaning would conflict with my urge to forge and strengthen the human relationships that formed that meaning. If the unexamined life was not worth living, was the unlived life worth examining?"

During the summer of his sophomore year, Kalanithi could either intern at a primate research center or cook at a lakeside camp. He chose camp and found "beauty manifest in lakes, mountains, people; richness in experience, conversation, friendships. . . . Every day felt full of life, and of the relationships that give life meaning."

Kalanithi earned an MA in English literature and later became a neurosurgeon. He died at thirty-seven from lung cancer but said, "It was literature that brought me back to life" during his illness.

6

BE CAREFUL
WHAT YOU AIM FOR.

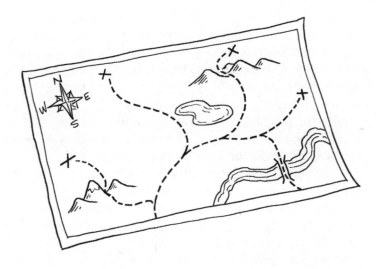

It is easy to get lost if you use the wrong map.

Randy Komisar, an entrepreneur who frequently lectures about business, calls the dominant approach to careers in Silicon Valley the Deferred Life Plan. It has two parts: "*Step one: Do what you have to do.* Then, eventually—*Step two: Do what you want to do.*"

The plan is deeply flawed. Komisar notes most ideas and start-ups in the valley fail, so the freedom associated with great wealth never materializes. People can spend years doing work bearing no relation to their interests or values and never reach step two.

Komisar concludes that people living a deferred life fail to realize an essential truth: "When all is said and done, the journey is the reward."

Designing Your Life is the title of a course and bestseller by Bill Burnett and Dave Evans. They reject the idea that life has a static destination. Rather, "Life design is a journey; let go of the end goal and focus on the process."

Burnett and Evans help students assess their views of life and work and imagine different futures. One exercise asks students to envision three lives: their current plan, the path they'd take if that option were not available, and "The Thing You'd Do or the Life You'd Live If Money or Image Were No Object."

The emphasis is on questioning and envisioning that lead to change and evolution. The result: "If you can see the connections between who you are, what you believe, and what you are doing, you will know when you are on course, when there is tension, when there might need to be some careful compromises, and when you are in need of a major course correction."

7
YOUR LIFE
HAS NO MEANING.

That's the first line of the first chapter of Professor Bernard Roth's book *The Achievement Habit*. It's soon followed by a sub-heading in bold letters: "**MY DAUGHTER HAS NO MEANING.**"

You might get the sense that you're on the road to nihilism here. But Roth's point is that intrinsic meaning does not exist. Relationships, work, experiences, and things have no meaning in and of themselves but only the meaning you choose to give them.

As Roth puts it, "Once you understand that you can *choose* what meaning and importance to place on something, you can also understand that it is you, not external circumstances, who determines the quality of your life."

You, not an external audience, are making the judgments. Roth points out, "In life, typically, the only one keeping a score-card of your successes and failures is you, and there are ample opportunities to learn the lessons you need to learn, even if you didn't get it right the first—or fifth—time."

Personal liberation is the last thing you might expect to learn from psychologist Phil Zimbardo, whose infamous Stanford Prison Experiment explored the effects of being assigned a role as a guard or prisoner in a simulation. Yet in *The Time Paradox*, Zimbardo (with John Boyd) urges people to exercise agency right now, saying, "What are you waiting for to bring purpose, clarity, and direction to your life? ... Time is what you make of it. Life is what you make of it."

Zimbardo and Boyd stress, "Finding purpose is a personal quest." How people choose to make their time matter will vary widely. As psychologists, they suggest that people sort out contending approaches to purpose by adopting a "Golden Rule of Time"—namely, "Use your time as you would like others to use theirs." The best time to start on that quest is now.

8
SOME WORSHIP
TO BELIEVE.

Churches on campus host tours, concerts, lectures, even yoga. And sometimes seekers.

When bell hooks came to college, she said, "[It did] not take me long to realize that the really hip people do not believe in god, that no one talks about religion."

But she went to Memorial Church daily, saying, "When I enter the sanctuary all the cares and hardships I feel daily fall away and there is for me here a place of peace. I come to church to pray. . . . To talk with god is to enter the place of mystery and possibility."

hooks became a professor famous for writing about race, class, and gender. When students asked what sustained her, she talked about spiritual life but said, "I had to find a way to talk about my choices that did not imply that they would be the correct or right choices for someone else."

Her message was clear: "My belief that God is love—that love is everything, our true destiny—sustains me. I affirm these beliefs through daily meditation and prayer, through contemplation and service, through worship and loving kindness."

In *How God Becomes Real,* anthropologist Tanya Luhrmann studies "whether people believe because they worship." She analyzes how "prayer and ritual and worship help people to shift from knowing in the abstract that the invisible other is real to feeling that gods and spirits are present in the moment, aware and willing to respond."

This is the faith frame, which she illustrates in this way: "You must be able to look at a glorious forest, and see not just an ecosystem but intentions. You must be able to be moved by a sunset, and to think not only of the structure of light, but of a maker."

Reflection, including prayer, doesn't bring perfection. But practice can bring perception, new ways of both seeing and experiencing the world.

9
THERE ARE SMART ATHEISTS AND SMART BELIEVERS ON CAMPUS.

But each often thinks the other may be missing out on life.

Neuroscientist Ben Barres came to atheism early: "Even in grade school I recognized that what I was being taught about God was not supported by evidence, was internally inconsistent, and made no sense."

Barres saw faith in a highly negative light, declaring, "I agree with those who have argued that it is a great crime to indoctrinate children with religious beliefs.... I wonder if such childhood indoctrination, by irreversibly affecting brain development, might have permanent effects on cognitive development, perhaps even impairing scientific thinking ability later in life."

Describing how bigotry affected him, Barres noted, "I was proud to be the first transgender scientist to be elected to the NAS [National Academy of Sciences] and was upset when the academy president refused to mention this in the NAS press release on the grounds that the academy 'had to deal with religious people.'"

In his twenties Paul Kalanithi embraced atheism. In the absence of proof, it was "unreasonable to *believe* in God."

Eventually this neurosurgeon changed his mind, saying, "Science may provide the most useful way to organize empirical, reproducible data, but its power to do so is predicated on its inability to grasp the most central aspects of human life: hope, fear, love, hate, beauty, envy, honor, weakness, striving, suffering, virtue."

Kalanithi came to see metaphysical questions as an arena for revelation, not proof. Describing his own journey, he wrote, "I returned to the central values of Christianity—sacrifice, redemption, forgiveness—because I found them so compelling."

His advice was to acknowledge uncertainty: "Struggle toward the capital-*T* Truth, but recognize that the task is impossible—or that if a correct answer is possible, verification certainly is impossible."

10
HOW DO YOU LIVE
A LIFE OF MEANING
AND PURPOSE?

Intentionally.

When professor of education William Damon studied people engaged in socially valuable work, he was "struck by how vividly these people were able to answer our questions about what they were trying to accomplish and why. An elevated purpose was always on their minds, driving their daily efforts. This purpose . . . gave them energy; it gave them satisfaction when they accomplished their goals; it gave them persistence when they ran into obstacles."

Damon defined "life purpose" as "the final answer to the question *Why? Why* are you doing this? *Why* does it matter to you? *Why* is it important?"

How people answer those questions varies. Damon notes that most people believe their work is meaningful for different reasons: "Perhaps because it helps others, perhaps because it contributes to society, perhaps because it affords a means of self-expression and personal growth, or perhaps because it provides a living for their families."

Swimming led Katie Ledecky to four Olympics, nine gold medals, and fame.

It also led her to schools and hospitals.

Veterans at Walter Reed National Military Medical Center lit up when she placed an Olympic gold medal around their necks. Ledecky says, "When I visit the kids at Children's National Hospital, the power of the gold medal is even stronger. They see the awards like a superhero accessory and love posing for photos wearing them."

Ledecky values the work and achievements that led to swimming fame. "But it is equally important to me," she notes, "to be seen as a kind, caring person who helped people, was nice to children, and was a good neighbor; someone who took my work seriously and was a reliable teammate throughout the years."

The good news is that you don't need to have a gold medal to help others. You simply need to care.

STAY HUNGRY. STAY FOOLISH.

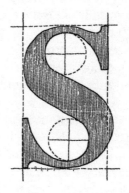

That's how Steve Jobs ended his famous 2005 commencement address, and those were words he lived by.

Jobs had dropped out of Reed College. He then dropped in on a calligraphy class, where he "learned about serif and sans serif typefaces, about varying the amount of space between different letter combinations, about what makes great typography great." Ten years later, he used that to give the Mac its distinctive typefaces and fonts.

The cofounder of Apple, he was abruptly fired at age thirty. This proved liberating: "I still loved what I did. . . . The heaviness of being successful was replaced by the lightness of being a beginner again, less sure of everything. It freed me to enter one of the most creative periods of my life." He founded another computer company, started Pixar (home of *Toy Story*), and met his future wife, Laurene Powell.

The moral for Jobs: "Don't settle."

Stewart Brand early in life displayed a spirit of restlessness and innovation in Silicon Valley.

A prophet in many fields—the counterculture, environmentalism, and the digital world—Brand expressed his aversion to everydayness in his journal. Entries include the following:

> When it comes to the point you're doing it mainly for the money, take steps toward moving on. . . . At a minimum, pick up something else you aren't doing for the money.

> Most of adulthood and its skills consists of adventure prevention.

Five years after graduating from college, Brand wrote these words in the journal: "Stay hungry. Stay foolish."

The phrase became a mantra when he put it on the back cover of the *Whole Earth Epilog*, which featured an early morning picture of a rural open road. The message clicked for a young Steve Jobs, who said after reading it, "I have always wished that for myself."

BE HERE NOW.

Sometimes you need to stop talking to yourself.

Being present requires stilling many thoughts. Gil Fronsdal, a PhD in religious studies, teaches how to be mindful of the present through meditation. He describes mindfulness as "training in how not to be lost in thoughts, opinions, and reactivity. It is also training in how to see things as they really are, as opposed to seeing them through the often distorted lens of preconceived ideas and interpretations."

Fronsdal notes a focus on breathing can center you: "By repeatedly coming back to rest in the breath, we are countering the strong forces of distraction. This trains the mind, heart, and body to become settled and unified on one thing, at one place, at one time."

Nancy Hamilton, who has an MA in East Asian studies, teaches how the Japanese way of tea connects people to the present. She describes this as

> attention to detail—in tea practice we are told, "your heart is in your fingertips." What am I touching now; what am I holding; what am I making; what am I doing. Put my heart into it. Attend to it with the gaze of my eyes and my heart. Not just some of it, all of it. Checking email while in a Zoom meeting? No. Killing two birds with one stone? No. Listening while worrying I will forget the point I am hoping to make? No. Put your heart into it—all of it. Your whole heart, without holding back, leaving no trace.

Sharing tea promotes connection and awareness:

> By devoting our full attention to the details of our contact here—this tea bowl, this scoop of water, this snap of the cloth—the heart is able to open and take in those around us with the same attitude of care.

REFLECTION–
WHAT MATTERS AND WHY.

No existential thoughts during exam period.

That's advice I offer during midterms and finals weeks. Students stressed by the prospect of exams start to question why they're struggling, what the payoffs to learning are, and where college will lead them in terms of careers. Those are important questions, but not ones to explore while stressed.

The night before my first college test, I tried to relax by calculating the percentage of all the grades I would get over the next four years that test would account for. The morning of my graduate school general exams, I threw up. I know from experience that when you're feeling pressure is not the time to demand answers from yourself about what matters to you and why.

A better approach is to recognize that college is part of a lifelong experiment, where you get to absorb new ideas and explore new experiences and test out alternate approaches to life. You get to examine what's important in life, write your own script, balance action and contemplation, and choose what's meaningful.

You won't find answers to these questions from a set of philosophy flash cards. Instead, you'll gather insights from many sources: talks with friends, interactions in extracurriculars, and readings and discussions in courses. To make progress, you need to be deliberative. That means taking the time to ask what you're learning about life, to reflect on what you're doing, and to think about how your beliefs and actions are changing based on these experiences.

This book opens with lessons about meaning not because you need to answer these before you can move on to other aspects of college. As you make your way through school, you have a unique chance to think through what matters to you. What's distinctive about this time in your life is that you're surrounded by others faced with similar questions, have time to talk about these challenges, and have access to courses and professors focused on these topics.

When I started college, I hoped to answer three questions: How should I live my life? What's the best form of government? Does God exist?

Spoiler alert: I found provisional but not definitive answers to those questions in college, and my replies keep evolving. That is one of the advantages of a liberal arts education. It instills a commitment to keeping an open mind and willingness to update your understanding as life gives you new information.

On how to live life, I learned a great deal in school from reading novels and essays by Walker Percy, Flannery O'Connor, and Ralph Ellison. Falling in love and traveling with friends also helped. My current answer involves putting family first and doing work that benefits other people.

On government, reading Tocqueville's *Democracy in America* convinced me that a democracy based on self-interest well understood is the ideal. Editing a political magazine and working on campaigns reinforced that lesson.

On religion, courses I took on moral and social inquiry and on the literature of religious reflection pointed me toward a yes. Experiences after college, such as having children and teaching them in Sunday school, also point to a yes. On any given day, though, I identify more as a seeker than an adherent.

Those are my answers. Yours will vary. The good news is that if you're confused and questioning, that is the best way to approach college. Knowing what you don't know will help you set out to find what you need, including a sense of what matters to you and why.

PURPOSE

13
CHOOSING YOUR MAJOR IS NOT CHOOSING YOUR CAREER.

You have more freedom than you think.

In a survey of employers, 93 percent agreed, "A candidate's demonstrated capacity to think critically, communicate clearly, & solve complex problems is more important than their undergraduate major."

When economists at the Federal Reserve looked at undergraduate degree holders, they found only "27% of undergraduate degree holders are working in a job that is directly related to their college major." A majority of accounting majors do go into accounting, and many architecture majors end up in that field. Yet for most majors, there is not a direct pipeline from classes to career.

The nature of work is changing, which means the job you'll hold fifteen years from now may not have been invented. People are changing gears too. On average, people work more than twelve different jobs between ages eighteen and fifty-six.

A university career office points out what's not changing: "Every major has transferable skills and knowledge that will be marketable to employers and there are always ways to gain additional industry skills and knowledge outside of your major."

Parents often believe otherwise.

Issa Rae told her father she would major in political science as a pathway to law school. When it came time to explain why she wanted to major in political science, her only answer was "because my dad wanted me to." So she chose a different major.

When her father discovered this at her college graduation, he yelled, "African American Studies?! You may as well have majored in FLOWERS!"

Issa Rae did not become a lawyer. Instead, she followed her interests. Her memoir, *The Misadventures of Awkward Black Girl*, became a bestseller; her HBO series, *Insecure*, garnered critical acclaim; and millions know more about life and love because of her commitment to storytelling.

14
STUDY WHAT'S INTERESTING.

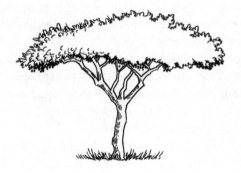

Learning is discovery. Sometimes what you find is what fascinates you.

In college Robert Sapolsky became intrigued by how emotions can affect your health. He particularly wanted to study stress-related disease. That ultimately led him to pursue decades of research about the behavior of baboons in the Kenyan grasslands.

Sapolsky chose baboons because they "live in big, complex social groups." He noted, "Baboons work maybe four hours a day to feed themselves. . . . [They] have about a half dozen solid hours of sunlight a day to devote to being rotten to each other."

Driven by his interest in stress and other emotions, he studied "who was doing what with whom—fights, trysts and friendships, alliances and dalliances." By studying changes in baboons' bodies, he was able to pursue deep questions about how differences in behavior translated into "individual differences in how their bodies were working."

When Guy Kawasaki picked courses in college, it all came down to money.

His strategy was simple: "I looked at what fields had the greatest job opportunities and prepared myself for them." But looking back on this approach, he now believes, "This was braindead. There are so many ways to make a living in the world; it doesn't matter that you've taken all the 'right' courses."

Kawasaki thrived in the tech world and experienced how teams with people with many different academic interests were successful. Giving advice to those headed to college, Kawasaki says, "Pursuing joy . . . will translate into one thing over the next few years for you. Study what you love."

Finding what you're interested in requires experimentation and approaching college with a sense of adventure. As Kawasaki notes, "One of the biggest mistakes you can make in life is to accept the known and resist the unknown."

DON'T LET PASSION BE YOUR ONLY GUIDE.

If you lack a central passion in college, you're in good company.

Psychologist William Damon has found in his research that "only about one in five young people in the 12–22-year age range express a clear vision of where they want to go, what they want to accomplish in life, and why."

The good news is that purpose develops over time. Damon notes, "The great majority of American workers do believe that their work is meaningful."

When Dr. Atul Gawande gave a graduation address, he talked about becoming a surgeon, author, and public health advocate:

> People say, "Follow your passion." But how many of you know what that is? I didn't. I had my share of enthusiasms, but sitting where you are, I wouldn't have called any my passion. I had no idea which would endure and which would fade.

Gawande had experimented in college. He cohosted a radio program, volunteered in politics, and learned to play guitar. He felt most energized working in the lab and talking politics with friends.

As a doctor he continued to try different career options. He counseled people to say yes to opportunities before forty so they could learn about themselves:

> In your formative years, you don't know—you can't know—what will ultimately matter to you, what will grab you by the shoulders and awaken you and stay with you. So you have to be open to trying stuff—to saying yes. As you do, pay attention to what fuels you and what doesn't. You want to pull apart the experience and figure out *specifically* what lifted you up and what sapped you. And then you want to do all you can to organize your life to do more of the first and less of the second.

16

BE OPEN TO THE FLOW.

Nirvana does not have an on-off switch. But it does have an on-ramp.

Dr. Emma Seppala, science director of the Center for Compassion and Altruism Research and Education, summarizes how this works:

> Research by Mihaly Csikszentmihalyi suggests that when you are completely immersed in an activity, you experience a highly energized and pure state of joy he calls *flow*. Flow occurs when you are 100 percent involved in an activity that is challenging enough to engage you (but not so challenging that it would take days to figure out). It is a state in which you are fully in the present moment, and it produces great pleasure.

Being in the moment leads to happiness but not from a simple choice to be happy. It comes from immersion in activity.

Athletes and academics call this being in the zone.

Sami Jo Small experienced both versions in college.

Small was on the track-and-field team and played men's hockey. Also during college, she was a goalie on the Canadian National Women's Hockey team. She ultimately played on teams that won three Olympic medals and five world championships.

Describing life in the net, she said, "No time to spare, I refocus on the next shooter. There's always another shooter, another opportunity. Each situation is different, but on every shot, I learn something new, building up a catalogue of techniques. Every moment leads into the next."

Small was premed. Then she took Mechanical Engineering 101, which she said "was a lot of work and kept me up all hours, but I loved every minute of it." Small switched to engineering. For her senior project, she wrote that she "designed upper-body goal tending equipment for women that helped me win a World Championship." She concluded, "I was hooked."

17

READ A NOVEL.

Sometimes your day is better if it's fictional.

English professors rarely champion efficiency. But Professor Blakey Vermeule, author of *Why Do We Care about Literary Characters?* praises novels as labor-saving devices. Fiction allows you to read minds and see patterns. As she notes, "Now after half a lifetime teaching literature, I walk around inside a vast pantheon of fictional people. I draw on their experiences—occasionally, a fictional character saves me from having to learn something the long, hard way."

Before there was Fortnite or the Metaverse, novels offered escape and guidance at the same time.

"Novels are the ultimate experience machines," Vermeule says. "They help you learn about your fellow creatures, what we go through, how highly sensitive we are, and what makes us tick. You really can't put anything over on George Eliot, Flaubert, or Leo Tolstoy. They've seen it all and then some."

Shankar Vedantam helps National Public Radio listeners think about human behavior through his *Hidden Brain* program and podcast. Describing how he reacted to great novels or stellar movies, Vedantam says, "I simultaneously know that the emotions I experienced were powerful and moving—*and real.*"

He makes the case that fiction can convey important truths: "Anna Karenina and Daenerys Targaryen and the old man who went fishing in the ocean and caught a fish that was too big for him never existed, but what *I* experience as I read or watch their stories *is real.* It brings me in touch with my hopes and fears, it makes me see things in a new way. It reminds me of the potential for horror that lies inside me, and the potential for greatness, too."

18

AND A HISTORY.

Your life's journey is unique. But its contours and challenges are familiar.

When John Hennessy was named a university president at age forty-seven, he hit the books. The professor of electrical engineering and computer science faced hard, empirical questions about power and decision-making. "So like any good researcher," he said, "I began reading books on leadership, especially biographies of great leaders."

Hennessy had always enjoyed reading histories: "Now I focused my reading on questions of leadership, historical breakthroughs, and historical disasters (especially those that were avoidable). I read the stories of great leaders to examine their habits, to understand what characteristics helped make them successful, to see how they prepared themselves for moments of crisis, and to understand how they handled success and—perhaps more important—failure."

A gifted engineering researcher, he saw the outcomes of others' actions as experiments to learn from: "Literature, biographies, and histories—they're like laboratories in which we can examine and learn critical lessons without having to live the difficulties ourselves."

Uses of history can also invite misuse.

Sam Wineburg, professor of education and history, warns politics can warp versions of the past offered to students: "History as truth, issued from the left or the right, abhors shades of gray. It seeks to stamp out the democratic insight that people of goodwill can see the same thing and come to different conclusions. It imputes the basest of motives to those who view the world from a different perch."

Wineburg contrasts this with a historical approach that acknowledges complexities, makes room for doubts, and tolerates uncertainty. That approach to learning and the past can lead you to change your mind. He points out this also involves "the moral courage we need to revise our beliefs in the face of new evidence."

19

YOU HAVE A LIFETIME TO EARN AND LEARN.

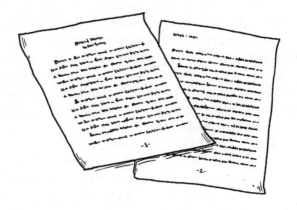

Your forty-year-old version can teach you about experience.

Economists recently calculated that starting salaries for computer science and engineering majors were 37 percent higher than those earned by social science or history majors. By age forty, this gap collapsed, with male social science and history majors earning higher average salaries. For women, those with applied STEM majors saw their salary premium over social science and history majors drop from about 50 percent at age twenty-five to 10 percent at forty.

Related work shows that in peak earning years, median annual earnings for humanities and social science majors were higher than those for professional and preprofessional majors, though engineering majors outearned both groups.

Why the drop in STEM salary advantages? Computer science and engineering teach highly valuable skills, but technical change can gradually make them obsolete. Humanities and social sciences develop critical thinking and problem-solving skills that contribute value across time. These majors are also a pathway to graduate degrees linked to leadership in business and law.

Carly Fiorina's path to becoming CEO of Hewlett-Packard included time as a college history major. She said, "I thought of college as a time for pure learning.... So I had the wonderful experience of studying the subjects that truly interested me."

Her "most valuable" class was *Christian, Islamic and Jewish Political Philosophies of the Middle Ages*. Each week she distilled hundreds of pages of readings into a two-page essay. She said, "Without knowing it at the time, I was developing an important management tool: how to understand and get from a seemingly overwhelming amount of information to the heart of the matter. And I was learning a leadership lesson: understanding and communicating the essence of things is difficult, takes a lot of thought, and has a big impact."

20
YOUR BEST COULD BEAT THE ODDS.

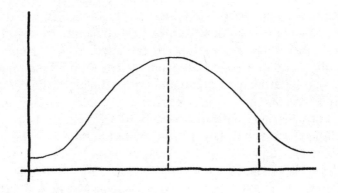

If you're thinking of selling, be sure to get the prices right.

Some students major in STEM for the best reasons: appreciation of quantitative rigor, desire to solve societal challenges, or interest in tech or scientific careers. Others pursue STEM coursework with reluctance. Parental pressure, FOMO (a fear of missing out) about internships, and high salaries lead students to pass on their preferred majors.

But if you follow your interests, you often do better. You think creatively, learn more, and truly excel. And that can pay off.

The median lifetime earnings of computer science majors are much greater than the median earnings for history, philosophy, or public administration and public policy majors. If you follow your interests, your achievements and success can land you in a different place on the distribution. At the 90th percentile of cumulative earnings by field, high-achieving computer science majors earn less over their careers than those who majored in history, philosophy, or public administration and public policy. Students in those fields often go to graduate school and end up in high-level management.

Describing her class choices as a public policy major in college, Rachel Maddow said, "I put together coursework that would help me be the best AIDS activist around."

Maddow followed a circuitous path: activist, barista, Rhodes Scholar, PhD in political science. As a cable host on MSNBC, author, and podcaster, she eventually reached millions and earned millions each year. Describing her career, she said, "Success is doing work that I'm proud of. It's about feeling like I am free to do what I want, and to say what I want, and to talk about things that I think are important, and to contribute something that wouldn't necessarily have been contributed had I not been the one working on it."

21

IF YOU'RE
DRIVING FOR SUCCESS,
YOU MAY MISS IT.

Your mileage may vary—in unexpected ways.

Consider France Córdova. After completing a BA in English, she was headed to graduate school in anthropology. Watching a story on public television about neutron stars, she wondered, "How do scientists know what they know?"

That question led her to pursue a PhD in physics. She became the "first to detect with a satellite dying stars in binary systems pulsing rapidly in X-ray light." Córdova said, "If you are 'plucky' (a combination of persistent and lucky) . . . [science provides] the immense thrill of discovery."

The noted astrophysicist later became director of the National Science Foundation. Describing her journey from literature to science, she said, "Keep your eyes out for side-streets and bike lanes. You may end up on an even more incredible journey than you had foreseen if you remain open to possibilities in unlikely places."

Reed Hastings almost stopped getting his MSCS in artificial intelligence to develop the foot mouse, designed to leave hands free for typing on the computer. When leg cramps and dirty floors defeated this innovation, he stayed in school.

At age thirty-seven, he founded Netflix. Describing himself as "more tortoise than hare," he advised graduates, "Maybe your path won't be clear, or you'll keep starting over in different areas. . . . If you're a tortoise, embrace it. Collect experiences and wisdom that will serve you later on."

After Hastings graduated from college, he taught math as a Peace Corps volunteer. He credited this time for giving him "the resilience and empathy to be a better CEO." He declared, "If you're a tortoise—emotionally, economically, intellectually, artistically, or otherwise—don't despair. You have the rest of your life to create the inventions and the stories that the world needs."

REFLECTION–
WHAT TO STUDY.

When you're navigating majors and courses, don't let fear take the wheel.

To get into college, you likely wrote essays that conveyed a strong sense of self and plans for the future.

Yet once you arrive on campus, especially at liberal arts schools, many academic advisors hope you'll consider changing the answers you spent so much time composing. This is a unique time in your life, a chance to question what you've assumed about your life's trajectory. The questions start coming fast, beginning with what you think you'll major in.

When I talk with first-year students, I'm struck by how often their reasoning focuses on negative outcomes. They don't want to disappoint their parents. They look at popular majors on campus and are overcome by FOMO. Tales of high starting salaries can steer students into particular majors, even if the courses don't seem inspiring or interesting.

If you're a hammer, everything looks like a nail. If you're a student, everything can look like a test. The selection of a major may look like another decision to ace. But it's not.

Data from employer surveys and alumni careers tell the same story. With a few exceptions, your major will not define your career. The market cares about whether you've developed critical thinking skills. Can you spot a problem, gather information, analyze options, and communicate possible solutions? Those are skills you can develop across many fields, meaning there is no one best answer to the question of what you should major in.

Even if you're choosing courses with an eye toward GPAs and graduate school, the good news is that majoring in what you're interested in can pay off. If you take courses you find inherently interesting, you'll often work harder, think more creatively, and excel.

If you don't have a driving passion, you're actually in the majority. You may in the coming years find something you're deeply driven by, but that is not a prerequisite for success or fulfillment. As William Damon notes, people find their work meaningful for many reasons, including its impact on others, its opportunity for self-expression, or the support it provides for their families.

As you struggle to adjust to college and make decisions about courses, it can be hard to know what's going on. Is it you, the specific college you've chosen, or college life in general that is generating challenges?

You only start college once, so the default may seem to be that the problem lies with you. Since I've taught thousands of students, I can tell you that the challenges relate more to general adjustment to college than the particulars of your life. If you choose courses where you read novels or histories, you'll find additional consolation in recognizing your ideas and feelings being voiced by others in fiction or the past.

I arrived at college deeply interested in government but ruled out a career in politics because I had a fear of public speaking. Medicine seemed like the ideal career, since I would be talking with one person at a time and helping them. So I started out as premed.

To fulfill a distribution requirement, I took economics. I enjoyed its relevance to policy issues, predictive power, and potential to change laws and lives. I ended up majoring in it and getting a PhD. I still don't like public speaking, but as a professor I enjoy teaching because I care about ideas and about students.

I'm lucky fear did not end up driving my choice of majors. I hope a sense of freedom and excitement ends up driving your selection of courses.

22
KEEP A
FAILURE RESUME.

Getting it right involves getting it wrong.

That's a central theme of Professor Tina Seelig's classes on creativity and entrepreneurship. Seelig requires her students to compose a failure resume "that summarizes all their biggest screwups—personal, professional, and academic. For every failure, each student must describe what he or she learned from that experience."

Seelig's own failure resume includes:

NOT DOING MY BEST: The first two years of college I didn't put my focused effort into all my courses. I missed the chance to extract the most value from the classes— a chance I can't get back.

AVOIDING CONFLICTS: I had a boyfriend in college, and as we closed in on graduation, we were both stressed about where we were going next. Instead of dealing with the questions about our future directly, I blew up the relationship. I wish I had been able to talk honestly about what was going on.

Even, or especially, when it's a matter of life and death, failure is instructive.

Dr. Atul Gawande studies system errors. Within hospitals, failures can arise from ignorance (partial understanding) and ineptitude (poor application of knowledge). When he devised a checklist for doctors and nurses to use before surgery and tested it in the field, he found significant drops in complications and patient deaths. Simple reminders acted as a "cognitive net. They catch mental flaws inherent in all of us—flaws of memory and attention and thoroughness."

Gawande notes that academic hospitals often have a weekly Morbidity and Mortality Conference, where doctors "gather behind closed doors to review the mistakes, untoward events, and deaths that occurred on their watch, determine responsibility, and figure out what to do differently next time."

What's acknowledged: "We are all, whatever we do, in the hands of flawed human beings."

23
GROW A
GROWTH MINDSET.

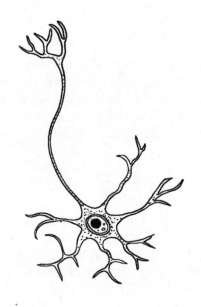

You don't have anything to prove.

But psychologist Carol Dweck knows people often feel they do. "Believing that your qualities are carved in stone—the *fixed mindset*—creates an urgency to prove yourself over and over," she says. Dweck contrasts this with the "*growth mindset . . .* based on the belief that your basic qualities are things you can cultivate through your efforts, your strategies, and help from others."

A fixed mindset leads to anxiety and avoidance of challenges, while "the passion for stretching yourself and sticking to it, even (or especially) when it's not going well, is the hallmark of the growth mindset."

You choose your mindset, influenced by circumstances. To help students see what triggers a fixed mindset, Dweck asks them to give it a name.

One student replied, "Meet Gertrude, my cagey, histrionic, self-aggrandizing fixed-mindset persona. . . . She detests hard work, second place, and imperfections."

Education school professor Jo Boaler gets in your head. She notes, "Every time we learn, our brains form, strengthen, or connect neural pathways." These pathways get stronger "when people are working at the edge of their understanding, making mistake after mistake in difficult circumstances, correcting mistakes, moving on and making more mistakes—constantly pushing themselves with difficult material."

She reports that students labeled "smart" are sometimes damaged: "The reason it makes them vulnerable is that if they believe they are 'smart' but then struggle with some difficult work, that feeling of struggle is devastating. It causes them to feel they are not smart after all and give up or drop out."

Fear of revealing their lack of knowledge leads to silence. As one student put it, "If I grew up in a world where no one was labeled as gifted, I would have asked a lot more questions."

24
GO AFTER
HARD CHALLENGES.

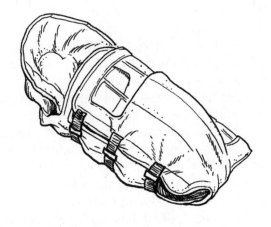

Sometimes it is life or death.

When four students came together in the course Design for Extreme Affordability, their challenge was to create a low-cost baby incubator for hospitals in developing countries.

They eventually learned low-birth-weight babies were not making it from rural areas to hospitals. They faced a choice: design for a hospital or for mothers in hard-to-reach areas.

One student remembers, "Some people on the team wanted to do the more remote setting. . . . Others . . . wanted to do something that could actually get finished by the end of class."

Their TA, Sarah Stein Greenberg, now the executive director of the Hasso Plattner Institute of Design (a.k.a. the Stanford d.school), advised, "You know, given a choice, I'd say go after the hard challenge. That's what puts the 'extreme' in Extreme Affordability."

They tackled the remote setting and developed what became the Embrace Portable Incubator, which to date has helped more than seven hundred thousand babies.

Myra Strober's life as a labor economist started with a hard challenge: her gender.

When she interviewed at Harvard's PhD program, a professor asked, "Why would you want to get a doctorate in economics if you're going to get married and have kids?" When she asked the chair of Berkeley economics why she was hired as a lecturer rather than assistant professor, he said, "It's because you have two young children, one not even a year old. We just don't know what's going to happen to you."

Eventually tenured at the Stanford Graduate School of Education, Strober became a leader in feminist economics. She studied the type of discrimination she'd surmounted. She concluded for "a woman to achieve power," she should be able to draw on "a favorable legal environment, a societal ideology that promotes gender equality, institutions that actively support her aspirations, and allies."

25

EXPECT SETBACKS.

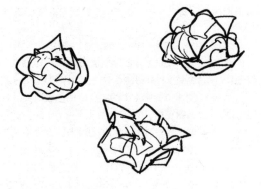

Learning starts when you see what you don't know.

Consider these reactions to early grades in college:

D in genetics: "My father wanted me to be a doctor ... but I couldn't get over that 'D' in genetics. So I found political science and history.... I also found the direction and then the vocation of my life."

C in freshman writing seminar: "I had never seen a letter like that on my report card. I was horrified."

C on first essay: "Big Exeter hero: know how to study, how to take essay exams. Hah!"

Put on academic probation: "'Can you bounce back?' I remember thinking, alone and in silence in my bedroom."

These students grew up to be Senator Dianne Feinstein, MacArthur genius award winner and *New Yorker* staff writer Dr. Atul Gawande, National Book Award winner Stewart Brand, and Stanford professor Albert M. Camarillo, whose pathbreaking work in Mexican American history and Chicano studies led him to serve as president of the Organization of American Historians.

In Charles Schwab's first quarter, he had a car, a fake ID, golf clubs, and a favorite tavern. He was "embracing the college experience with a full hug." He also nearly flunked out.

He dropped off the golf team, studied more, and rallied. He was dyslexic, though undiagnosed. He said, "I have always tried particularly hard to keep up, to tackle the things that were so hard for me but seemed so easy for everybody else."

His setbacks had an upside: "The positive side of dyslexia, thinking differently, more conceptually, helped me a lot in developing Schwab." The financial services company he went on to found now manages more than $9 trillion in assets.

26

BIAS TOWARD ACTION IS THE NEW *CARPE DIEM*.

At some point, planning stops and doing starts.

In a course called LaunchPad, where students create their own businesses, Akshay Kothari and Ankit Gupta decided to design an iPad news reader. They went to a Palo Alto café with a rough prototype, gathered feedback, and fine-tuned. The result was Pulse, an app they sold to LinkedIn, which incorporated it into the reading habits of millions.

Describing this creative process, Gupta observed, "It's not about just coming up with the one genius idea that solves the problem, but trying and failing at a hundred other solutions before arriving at the best one." Kothari's takeaway: "If I had an idea, I would just keep thinking about it in my mind, or I'd talk about it, but I wouldn't do anything about it. Now it feels natural to have an idea and then immediately build a prototype."

Richard Engel took a leap several weeks after graduating from college by moving to Cairo. He said, "I had no job lined up, no contacts, I spoke no Arabic, and I had about 2,000 dollars in my pocket. I packed two suitcases and left on a one-way ticket. I wanted to be a journalist and I thought the Middle East would become the story of my generation."

Engel was right. He covered wars in Lebanon, Libya, and Iraq; chronicled the Arab Spring; and was kidnapped (and escaped) in Syria. His award-winning reporting made him chief foreign correspondent for NBC News.

Sharing insights from this journey with graduating students, he said, "You have youth in abundance and there's nothing else worth having. You have smarts. So don't squander it by chasing the mundane allures of money and comfort. . . . Try something new, and then try it again."

27

BE CURIOUS.

Discovery starts with a willingness to wander.

Richard Levin has thought hard about what distinguishes colleges. He's a Stanford alum, parent, and former president of Yale. In a reunion class note, he described the university this way: "Independence, innovation, and entrepreneurship are prized. Students are irreverent, open, and curious.... Stanford is an invitation to self-discovery."

As a university president, Levin stressed the unique benefit of college life, saying, "You have four years—free from the pressures of career and family obligations that you will encounter later—to reflect deeply on the life you wish to lead and the values you wish to live by." He encouraged students to pursue four goals as undergrads: "to give free rein to your curiosity, to develop independent ideas, to remain open-minded in the face of evidence, and to prepare yourselves not only for lives of personal satisfaction and professional achievement but also for service to others."

Dudley Herschbach took risks to explore his interests in college. When a football coach said he could not take labs that conflicted with practice, he walked away from the team. He sampled courses widely, being willing to try fields he wasn't the best in. His philosophy: "You can explore the world, but you don't have to be superior in everything."

Each day he'd study from 9 a.m. to noon in the library, making outlines and losing himself "in ideas and stories, problems and solutions." He said that in taking classes across fields, people "meet different kinds of questions and wildly diverse criteria for evaluating answers.... We learn to challenge evidence and patiently puzzle out our own answers."

Following puzzles eventually led him to a PhD in chemistry and a Nobel Prize. Irreverence and excitement about science led him to guest star on *The Simpsons*.

28
QUESTION YOURSELF:
I LIKE, I WISH, WHAT IF?

Knowing what you need starts with asking what you want.

As executive director of the Stanford d.school, Sarah Stein Greenberg thinks hard about creativity, empathy, and leadership. She says, "If you want to make just one change to improve your work, your family, your team, or your organization, consider this"—ask what works, what doesn't, and what might.

Stein Greenberg notes this can be a solo endeavor, where "jotting down a list of personal likes and wishes after a meeting or an experience gives you a habit of viewing everything as both valuable and improvable." It can also be a group exercise, where you "invite everyone to reflect on the experience they've just had ... using a statement that begins with 'I like ...' or 'I wish....'" This reflection "demonstrates the value you place on making the work better."

With an MA in learning, design, and technology, Majo Molfino writes about women envisioning change. She says, "One of the more interesting phenomena I've discovered in my coaching ... is that it's very hard for us to be creative about our own lives.... We limit ourselves and say things like 'I couldn't possibly get away with that' or 'That's too crazy.'"

To get beyond the self-imposed constraints you might encounter when you try to imagine what might work differently in your life, Molfino recommends a particular type of brainstorming. She observes, "To get really good ideas, you need to generate a huge number of them. First ideas aren't usually good, and only a small percentage are actually interesting, so cast a wide net." Seeing the world a different way can come from a sense of abandon, since "wild ideas are how you get to innovative solutions. Don't be afraid to suggest weird and funky ideas."

29
LEARN A FIELD.

Going deep can take you far.

As a lesbian working on AIDS issues, Rachel Maddow was an outlier in college. She says, "I never felt like I really fit in, so I decided that as long as I'm here, I'd like to use the incredible resources of this place to accrue some assets, to try to build something that I could use in this fight that I felt ethically and culturally to be part of."

Her strategy was to "put together coursework that would help me be the best AIDS activist around. . . . I took statistics courses because I thought I needed to be better with the statistical part of the arguments, and I took philosophy courses because that was about rigor in argumentation. . . . I took history and politics because I wanted to understand the context of what I was doing in public policy, and I did a concentration in health policy."

Michael McFaul's deep dive in college into international relations was similarly inspired by public policy. He says, "As a freshman, I enrolled in first-year Russian and Intro to International Relations—because I thought Reagan was dangerous. . . . The Cold War seemed like it could become hot. I wanted to do something about it."

McFaul spent time as an undergraduate in the Soviet Union, first in a summer language program and then a semester in Moscow. Afterward, he "no longer believed that engagement between the two countries was enough." He said, "I started to consider an alternative theory: only democratic change inside the Soviet Union would allow our two governments and our two societies to come closer together."

Maddow and McFaul both went to Oxford as Rhodes Scholars and earned PhDs. Her expertise eventually led to award-winning journalism, his to outstanding public service as US ambassador to Russia.

30
DEVELOP CRITICAL THINKING SKILLS.

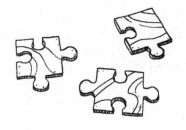

The best classes teach you how to think, not what to think.

As president of Harvard University, Derek Bok believed colleges should teach critical thinking skills. He defines those as "qualities of mind and habits of thought" that include "an ability to recognize and define problems clearly, to identify the arguments and interests on all sides of an issue, to gather relevant facts and appreciate their relevance, to perceive as many plausible solutions as possible, and to exercise good judgment in choosing the best of these alternatives."

Friends, seminars, and extracurriculars develop those skills. Bok also hopes people come to see that some outcomes and answers are uncertain, so that "even well-reasoned conclusions are best thought of as provisional, to be discarded if necessary when powerful contrary facts and arguments come to light."

Richard Levin majored in history in college and later earned a PhD in economics from Yale, where he eventually became president. Levin also sees a liberal education as developing "qualities of mind," including "the ability to think independently, to regard the world with curiosity and ask interesting questions, to subject the world to sustained and rigorous analysis, to use where needed the perspectives of more than one discipline, and to arrive at fresh, creative answers."

Challenging class discussions, open-ended paper assignments, and exam questions requiring analysis and argument teach you to reason. Levin notes, "This distinctive emphasis on critical thinking produces graduates who are intellectually flexible and open to new ideas, ... graduates who, in business, can convert new knowledge into new products and services and who, in government, can find innovative solutions to new challenges." Another benefit is that "the ability to think critically and independently" can free you "from prejudice, superstition, and dogma."

31

YOU MAY BE WRONG.

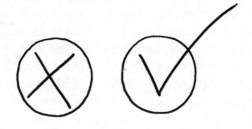

And they may be right.

Stephen L. Carter teaches at Yale Law School, where people argue for a living. He notes that true dialogue involves dialing back your ego, keeping an open mind, and being willing to change. He knows that's hard because "our senses of ourselves are deeply bound up with our senses of *this-I-believe*, whether our *this* involves a party affiliation, a commitment to nonviolence, a position on abortion, or even (especially!) our belief or nonbelief in God."

Real conversations open important beliefs to change. Carter urges you to avoid "the error of allowing others to speak only because we need to hear their views in order to be able to refute them." He argues in politics and other domains, we need to "allow ourselves the possibility of being persuaded by the other" party, person, or side.

How to acknowledge errors and make better decisions is the focus of *Decisive*, written by business school professor Chip Heath and his brother Dan. They point out the many ways you can go wrong in choosing. Confirmation bias leads you to focus on information that supports your beliefs. As you approach a decision, you narrow options too quickly, fail to question your assumptions, and are too confident about future events.

The Heaths pose simple questions to help avoid these errors. Instead of arguing with a friend about alternatives, ask yourself, "What would have to be true for this option to be the right answer?" Rather than committing to an option and digging in, they encourage you to ask, "What if our least favorite option were actually the best one? What data might convince us of that?"

In life, as in *Jeopardy*, putting answers in the form of a question can lead you to learn the unexpected.

32

WHAT IMPORTANT TRUTH DO FEW AGREE WITH YOU ON?

That's a hard question, requiring insight and a willingness to go against the grain.

And that's why Peter Thiel likes to ask it during job interviews. Thiel, who has a BA in philosophy and a law degree, is famously contrarian. He's also famously successful as an entrepreneur and investor. He cofounded PayPal and Palantir and invested early in Facebook and LinkedIn.

He asks tough questions because he's after change. He defines a start-up as "the largest group of people you can convince of a plan to build a different future." The way they do that is to "question received ideas and rethink business from scratch."

Thiel's own answer to his question is "Most people think the future of the world will be defined by globalization, but the truth is that technology matters more." Your answer could affect the ideas or opportunities you pursue.

Reid Hoffman agrees that disagreement fuels success.

As you would expect from the cofounder of LinkedIn, Hoffman argues that tapping your network is central to improving your ideas. He counsels founders, "Don't ask people, 'What do you think of my idea?' Ask them, 'What's wrong with my idea?'"

Pushing yourself to learn where you're wrong helps you get smarter quicker. Hoffman notes, "Thoughtful leaders thrive on disagreement because it gives them the information they need to improve their ideas before they reach the world." This can run against human nature because we all like praise. Hoffman points out, "Praise might make you feel good in the moment, but it doesn't actually help you succeed."

Seeing what won't work can help you find what will more quickly. Hoffman notes, "The earlier you can predict a 'Yes' in a field of 'Nos,' the bigger your opportunity."

33

TRUTH DEPENDS
ON ACCURACY.

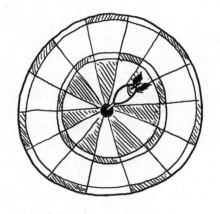

If you don't care about your work, why should someone else?

That's a question journalism professor Bill Woo posed to students. Woo urged them to produce accurate reporting. He said, "We are just a small journalism class. . . . But I want you to treat your work with the same care, the same concern for quality, the same respect for the abiding values and principles of our craft as if you worked for the finest paper on earth."

Woo acknowledged that time pressure, complexity, and uncertainty mean capturing the reality of a situation can be difficult. Yet he stressed, "Truth depends on accuracy. . . . We are dealing with facts and figures and quotes and direct observations that need to be accurate." That entails work and a focus on details. Woo insisted, "We must believe in what we write; we must care about it. If we do not, why should readers?"

Much of what you read or view each day is driven by concern with attention, not accuracy. Social media strives for engagement, which attracts likes and advertisers. Streaming services focus on entertainment and diversion, not enlightenment.

Jim Tankersley, a former student of Bill Woo, covers economic policy for the *New York Times*. He notes that market pressure leads some journalists to report using "the dramatic structure of a novel." Policy disputes are reduced to a battle between heroes and villains. He concludes, "It is a clean and easy and effective way to tell stories. But it is not, in my experience, an accurate reflection of how the world usually works."

Understanding and solving problems involves realistic assessments, which take effort. Stories of heroes and villains make life simpler. But Tankersley warns, "Our greatest heroes are almost always flawed. The people we call villains are sometimes not the bad guys at all."

34
PURSUE CRAZY IDEAS.

Sometimes you're the one who turns a long shot into a sure thing.

In a business school entrepreneurship class, Phil Knight saw the promise of importing running shoes from Japan. He became obsessed: "The idea interested me, then inspired me, then captivated me." The course consumed him: "I'd moved into the library, devoured everything I could find about importing and exporting, about starting a company."

When he presented his paper, there were zero questions from students. The professor liked the idea and gave him an A. Knight said he "pondered going to Japan, finding a shoe company, pitching *them* my Crazy Idea, in the hopes that they'd have a more enthusiastic reaction than my classmates."

He did go to Japan, and he made the pitch, "quoting my presentation at Stanford, verbatim, speaking lines and numbers I'd spent weeks and weeks researching." So began Knight's shoe company, Nike.

About her time as an undergraduate, Issa Rae says, "I wanted to be a writer and I wanted to pursue film, TV ... and I wanted to tell our stories—but I was also too scared to pursue it as anything but a hobby."

In her senior year, she enlisted friends to act in a series about being Black at Stanford called *Dorm Diaries*. The program's success on Facebook led her to "realize that Hollywood was wrong about there not being an audience for the stories I wanted to tell."

After Stanford, Issa Rae described herself as a "clumsy, frustrated, socially inept, recently graduated adult, looking for confirmation that [she] wasn't alone." But she tapped into Kickstarter and drew upon college friends to produce the YouTube series *The Misadventures of Awkward Black Girl*. The success of that production online made visible her talents and her audience, leading ultimately to her HBO series, *Insecure*.

35

WHAT WOULD YOU DO IF YOU COULD NOT FAIL?

That's the question that got Cory Booker unstuck.

In college, he had clear goals—"play varsity, get A's, and be deeply involved in public service." But in his first year in law school, he could not define what was next.

His mother set him straight. She asked, "If you knew for sure you would be successful, what would you do? Who would you be, how would you behave, how would you feel, how would you serve? Answer that question. Feel that. Act like that." She noted that if he did fail, he would be "wiser, stronger, and more capable."

That reframing reenergized Booker. It led to new questions: "If I were to do good for others, what would I need in order to excel? Whom would I need to meet?" The answers led to a life in politics.

Fear of failure can keep you focused on the credential ladder without asking whether you're headed where you want to go.

As a young alum working on Capitol Hill put it, "When people start looking for internships the tech companies, investment banks, and consulting firms are appealing because they have a structured application process, interview timeline, and path to a full-time job offer."

He noted that other career paths have less certainty, especially at the start: "Public service work, non-profit work, startups, and any organization that doesn't have a big HR department won't have this structure."

Graduating with a degree in economics, he turned down a highly paid job to pursue work in Congress. His first job was assembling binders for hearings. Eighteen months later, he was helping draft legislation.

Choosing a less-structured path means betting on yourself, but the gains in experience and satisfaction can be tremendous.

REFLECTION—
SAMPLE AND LEARN.

Sampling is life.

In college you're seeking new experiences. There are disciplines to explore, people from many different backgrounds to meet, a wide range of extracurriculars to pursue. If you're committed to learning, that means you'll make choices leading to unexpected outcomes. You may fail to grasp concepts, stretch but not reach a goal, start but not finish a project.

What you learn from failure determines your ultimate success. Learning comes from working on the edges of your abilities, from trying something new. When things don't work out the way you planned, thinking about what to do differently in the future is the way forward.

Those words are easy to read but can be hard to live by. You've likely been told that it's important to have a growth mindset or that failure is instructive. I find, though, that when it comes to making decisions in college, students want certainty they'll get the best possible outcome on the first try.

I try to counter the focus on being right all the time by urging students to think probabilistically about ideas, papers, jobs, and people.

When I was in graduate school, a professor revealed he stayed awake in seminar by repeatedly asking, "Why is what this person is saying wrong?" I prefer a different question: "What am I missing here?"

We all have ideas about how markets and politics work. Understanding how the world actually works is hard, so we default to assumptions and rules of thumb.

A subset of those are wrong. To learn which ones, try this experiment when you're talking about people or politics and reach a disagreement. Ask: How could I be wrong? What do they know that I don't understand?

The idea that you should get it right the first time can freeze you when you're trying to write a paper. I often ask students starting a new project to write three one-page memos. The first memo paragraph contains expected results, the second the methods used. The exercise of taking three stabs at a project frees you up so you realize there is not just one way to approach a topic.

When students are hesitant to commit to a summer internship or first job out of college, I stress that there is no such thing as a bad first job. You're sampling different approaches to work. You may learn what you love to do or, just as important, what you don't.

My first job after college was as a research assistant at a consulting firm. The work was always demanding, rarely challenging. But I learned three important things about myself from the experience: I am not motivated primarily by money. I don't like to work on questions defined by other people. And I don't like working in poorly managed groups.

Those lessons led me to a PhD, providing me with a life where I work on puzzles I find interesting whose solutions can have a positive effect on society.

I view my days as toggling between work that has a small probability of affecting a large number of people (research) and a large probability of affecting a small number of people (teaching). As a student, you face the same mix. On a given day, what you may discover could have a small probability of ultimately leading to big change: new ideas, products, or policies. You also can have a large probability of affecting a small number of people through how you navigate the day: calling your parents, emailing a mentor, or even making direct eye contact as you thank someone behind a counter.

CHOOSING

36
ACT LIKE A START-UP.

Do you work to live or live to work?

In *The Start-Up of You*, Reid Hoffman and Ben Casnocha argue that the principles of entrepreneurship apply readily to both work and life. In both you consider "your assets, your aspirations"; make plans and change them based on "feedback and lessons learned"; "build real, lasting relationships"; "find and create opportunities for yourself"; and "take on intelligent risk."

Central to both is the *pivot*, defined as "changing direction or changing your path to get somewhere *based on what you've learned along the way*."

Hoffman originally planned "to be an academic and public intellectual." But in graduate school he "discovered that academics end up writing for a scholarly elite of typically about fifty people.... My aspiration to have a broad impact on potentially millions of people clashed with the market realities of academia."

His pivot: "My new aim was to try to promote the workings of a good society via entrepreneurship and technology." Hoffman went on to start LinkedIn, where more than a billion members now manage their professional identities.

Dan Edelstein helped create the class Why College: Your Education and the Good Life with the hope that first-year students would pivot from a focus on money and career to a broader goal of "becoming a more interesting person."

Edelstein points out that a liberal education embraces curiosity, exposes complexities, and generates a sense of wonder—which he notes is "the source of friendship, happiness, and a good life."

And here's the good news: "The truth is that having a broad diversity of interests and insights on many topics will help win people over at work as well as in leisure.... The same skills make us desirable both as friends and as co-workers."

37

ACKNOWLEDGE LUCK.

Your stroke of good luck could be on a keyboard.

Marissa Mayer came to college as a premed. But something clicked when she took CS 105 Introduction to Computers. Her design of an exploding fireworks screensaver came in second in a class of three hundred, setting her on a pathway to major in symbolic systems and earn an MS in computer science.

In her final spring at university, hard work and intelligence yielded twelve job offers (including a position at the consulting firm McKinsey). Eating pasta while going through emails, she meant to delete a recruiter pitch. She missed the delete key and hit space, and that made all the difference.

Reading the email that popped up entitled "Work at Google?" she remembered her mentor talking about a search start-up by two PhD students named Sergey and Larry. She interviewed for the spot, became Google employee number twenty, and began a Silicon Valley career that led to being CEO of Yahoo.

Reed Hastings cofounded and led a company, Netflix, built on data and algorithms. And he's a firm believer in luck.

In a commencement address, he talked about the weak bonds between the "very lucky and the less lucky." He said, "By very lucky, I mean those born beautiful, healthy, athletic, intelligent, empathetic; those born in peaceful countries to caring parents and those who got bedtime stories read to them every night. Many of you, like me, have won several of those lotteries, and also have worked hard to build on that luck. So what is the duty of the more lucky to the less lucky?"

Stories about "rugged individualism," effort, and holding onto your gains leave out those with less luck. Hastings hopes that the next generation devises a moral narrative about a "common prosperity" rather than acceptance of life as a lottery.

38
EVERYONE FEELS
LIKE AN IMPOSTER.

When you're new, it's hard to feel like you belong.

Julian Castro was mayor of San Antonio at thirty-four, became the first Latino to keynote a Democratic National Convention, and served as Secretary of Housing and Urban Development in President Obama's cabinet. In 2019 he ran for the Democratic nomination for president.

All of this was ahead when he went to his first party at college. There was a keg and a sea of Solo cups. Castro, who did not drink, said he "felt out of place. This had nothing to do with drinking and everything to do with my confidence and image of myself."

He went to the bathroom, filled a cup, and "spent the next two hours at the party slowly sipping tap water." But that was the last time he did that: "I realized that I would be much better off just being myself around people. That way I'd attract friends who liked the real me, not some person I was trying to be."

On Condoleezza Rice's first morning on a new campus, she felt uneasy. She said, "As I made my way along the long colonnade flanked with sandstone columns, I felt a level of insecurity that I'd never felt before and have never felt since. I'd been slowly climbing out of the obscurity of the University of Denver, but I couldn't quite believe that I was about to become a doctoral fellow at Stanford. A part of me wondered if the university had made a mistake."

Rice became a tenured professor. When she was offered the provost's job at thirty-eight, she reports, "As I made my way back to my office, memories flooded back of walking along the same colonnade as an insecure graduate student . . . I knew that I'd say yes and become provost."

39

LIFE IS NOT LINEAR.

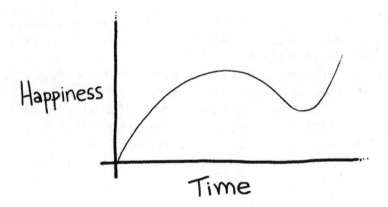

Starting college can feel like a step backward.

As one senior noted, "In high school getting into a good college was always the goal so it was easy to find purpose, but once I got in I felt lost and it was much more difficult to know what to do."

He considered going with the goals he described in his admission essays. Yet he learned, "It's easy and comfortable to stick to preconceived notions about yourself, but if you do you may find that you regret not trying different things. You never have more freedom to explore than in college, so take advantage of the time while you can."

He rejected others' expectations and comparisons to peers as guides, noting, "The quicker you let go of these external factors and focus on yourself the quicker you can start making progress towards the person you want to become."

Melissa A. Hosek sees a U-shaped pattern of happiness among her first-year students.

She notes the transition to college "consists of a honeymoon phase, a gradual decline, a 'low' of frustration, and then an eventual upswing in sentiment." Her takeaway for students: "If you aren't feeling 100% wonderful all the time in your new setting, that's normal! Most importantly, it *will* get better! All you need is some self-compassion and time."

Hosek knows this from experience. Homesick at college, she says, "[I] began to wonder if something was wrong with me ... wasn't college supposed to be the best years of my life? Wasn't everyone supposed to be happy and wonderful all the time? Wasn't I supposed to instantly find my new best friends? As it turns out, this didn't happen for me right away ... but it got better!"

She reminds students that "frustration, loneliness, and disappointment are part of big life transitions," and with support and self-compassion, they will eventually thrive.

40
DITCH THE
DUCK SYNDROME.

Working to exhaustion is not a pathway to success or happiness.

But that route has a name—the Duck Syndrome. Dr. Emma Seppala observes, "On the surface, the students look like peaceful ducks, serenely gliding along in the sun, contentedly basking in the splendor and grace of their success. However, if you look under the surface, there is a dark underside: the ducks' legs are furiously pedaling as they struggle to stay afloat and to keep moving."

Seppala says students have false ideas about the nature of success: "Never stop accomplishing. . . . You can't have success without stress. . . . Persevere at all costs." She highlights research showing how fulfillment comes from alternative strategies: "Instead of always thinking about what's next on your to-do list, focus on the task or conversation at hand. . . . Instead of engaging in exhausting thoughts and emotions, learn to manage your stamina by remaining calm and centered."

Jenny Odell, who's taught digital art in college classes, describes Duck Syndrome as "essentially a joke about isolated struggle in an atmosphere obsessed with performance." She notes how economic precarity perceived by students produces anxiety. The result: "Fear renders young people less able to concentrate individually or collectively. An atomized and competitive atmosphere obstructs individual attention because everything else disappears in a fearful and myopic battle for stability."

The remedy she offers is simple and challenging. She imagines putting her phone down, walking to a park, and observing with her full attention. She admits, "Seen from the point of view of forward-pressing, productive time, this behavior would appear delinquent. . . . But from the point of view of the place, I'd look like someone who was finally paying it attention. And from the point of view of myself . . . I would know that I spent that day on Earth."

41

EXPECT PAIN, LONELINESS, AND SADNESS.

Achievement can go hand in hand with sadness.

As an English major, bell hooks began writing a pathbreaking book entitled *Ain't I a Woman: Black Women and Feminism*. Describing her time as an undergraduate, she wrote,

> Sadness soaks my body like that moment when you are caught unexpectedly in a rain shower and are wet through and through. When I feel like I can't take it any more— when I am falling into the abyss, I go to the pastures on campus to be near horses, the sun, the smell of manure. I ... dream of meadows, of a place of contentment where all my dreams can be fulfilled.

Describing another way forward from unhappiness, hooks quotes T. H. White's character Merlin in *The Once and Future King*: "The best thing for being sad is to learn something. That is the only thing that never fails."

In the eye of the camera, MSNBC host Rachel Maddow is confident, cogent, and fluid.

But behind the scenes, she may be hurting. As someone with cyclical depression, she can at times "lose [her] will and [her] ability to focus." Acknowledging this with a hope that her experience can help reach others, she says, "The way I experience depression is a real closing off from the world.... It's like somebody hits the mute button. It's very lonely, and it can be alienating."

What works for Maddow is to recognize that this will and does happen to her. She says of her wife, Susan, "[She] reminds me that I'm having an episode and that it's temporary and I shouldn't allow it to stop my life." Summarizing her experience, Maddow says, "I can't make the depression go away, but I can be cognizant of it."

42

NEVER MISS AN OPPORTUNITY TO BE FABULOUS.

That's the advice Professor Tina Seelig offers on the first day of class. She promises to excel as a teacher, and she wants her students to aim for the extraordinary.

The result: "The students consistently deliver more than I or they ever imagined. They embrace the idea of being fabulous with remarkable enthusiasm and raise the bar repeatedly as the quarter progresses.... I now know that everyone is just waiting to get this instruction. They're hungry for permission to do their very best."

Classes can be an exercise in checking boxes, meeting expectations, and moving on to a degree. But not Tina Seelig's courses. She challenges students to "Give Yourself Permission," noting, "By that I mean, give yourself permission to challenge assumptions, to look at the world with fresh eyes, to experiment, to fail, to plot your own course, and to test the limits of your abilities."

To excel as an actor, Sterling K. Brown set aside fear. A quote from Marianne Williamson that changed his life was this:

> Our deepest fear is not that we are inadequate. Our deepest fear is that we are powerful beyond measure. It is our light, not our darkness, that frightens us most. We ask ourselves, "Who am I to be brilliant, gorgeous, talented, and famous?" Actually, who are you not to be?

When he was reluctant to appear foolish in a play in grad school, an instructor said, "It's not about you, Sterling. We're all learning from your experience." Brown came to see that taking risks and pursuing excellence inspires others to do the same. Describing his willingness to trade safety for experience, he says, "If all of my life is comfortable and convenient, I rob myself of the opportunity to grow, to stretch, to expand."

43

IT'S THE JOURNEY, NOT THE DESTINATION.

That's the title and conclusion of an article by business school professors Szu-Chi Huang and Jennifer Aaker.

Across six studies on topics ranging from dieting to exercising to learning, they prompted some participants to see the activity as a journey and others to focus on the end goal. Those empowered by the journey metaphor were more likely to talk about their experience as one of personal growth and change.

Huang and Aaker also found a continuing impact of the metaphor. After a goal was achieved, those prompted to see the activity as a journey were more likely to continue the choices that got them to the goal. Those who had been led to see the goal simply as a destination to achieve were less likely to keep on with the activities that got them there.

On the day that Deborah Liu started at Facebook, she resolved to become part of the "M-Team," the "small group of people who led the company." After she reached that goal, she found herself asking, "Is this all there is?"

Liu had seen herself as climbing a career ladder. But she realized, "The ladder is infinite if you are willing to climb it, and there is never a top rung. The reward for climbing higher is seeing what you haven't yet accomplished. But what I didn't realize then was that someone else had constructed the ladder, and I was living by their definition of success, not mine."

She chose to follow her own path and detours, eventually becoming CEO of Ancestry. The road map she set: "I want to leave people better for having met me. I am a problem solver, connector, and creator, so I will use these skills to live with no regrets."

44
GET S'MORE
OUT OF LIFE.

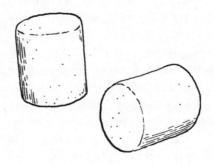

The most famous college test happened at the campus nursery school.

Psychologist Walter Mischel offered preschoolers a marshmallow right away, or two marshmallows if they could wait about twenty minutes. Those who were able to delay their gratification got more treats. Mischel also found that later in life, they had better SAT scores, possessed a higher sense of self-worth, and navigated stress more easily.

The good news from Mischel's research is "the ability to delay immediate gratification for the sake of future consequences is an acquirable cognitive skill." If you make an implementation plan where you identify your response, then you can have more self-control.

Knowing what you will do is liberating and habit forming. Thinking ahead of time about how to complete sentences starting with "when I'm craving something, when I'm bored, when I'm anxious, when I'm angry" makes it more likely you'll achieve your goals.

Psychologist B. J. Fogg agrees successful habits can be built by design. The keys: "Stop judging yourself. Take your aspirations and break them down into tiny behaviors."

Fogg praises small steps. He notes, "Tiny allows you to get real with yourself and your life. Tiny allows you to start *right now*." His "Tiny Habits for Success in College" includes these plans:

After I hear my alarm, I will put one foot on the floor and try to wake up.

After I walk into the library, I will sit at a table in the far corner away from other people.

After I get out my homework assignment, I will put my phone on airplane mode.

After I sit down for class with my laptop, I will turn off Wi-Fi.

After any professor sends me an e-mail, I will respond immediately even if it's just this: "Got it. Thank you."

45
HAVE YOUR CALENDAR REFLECT YOUR VALUES.

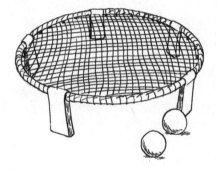

Elementary school got it right—you should schedule time for play.

Before getting an MA in journalism, Simone Stolzoff worked at a tech start-up. The job was all-consuming. He found, "Life became work, and work became a series of rinse-and-repeat days that felt indistinguishable from one another."

He eventually wrote a book entitled *The Good Enough Job: Reclaiming Life from Work*. He describes how some people consciously schedule time each week "when work is not an option" and guard that time on their calendar.

Time to protect takes many forms: friendships, hobbies, reading, sports. A favorite for Stolzoff is play. He notes, "Play is a natural antidote to workism.... Like rest, play can be a source of rejuvenation.... Play helps us remember that we exist to do more than just produce."

Did you really do it? That's the question MBA alum Nir Eyal asks when he looks over the previous week's schedule and evaluates what he did. Sometimes a phone call, a text, an online story will divert attention and disrupt plans.

Eyal urges you to look at the past week and ask yourself, "Are there changes I can make to my calendar that will give me the time I need to better live out my values?"

In *Indistractable: How to Control Your Attention and Choose Your Life*, Eyal reminds you that people are not an afterthought: "A lack of close friendships may be hazardous to your health. Ensure you maintain important relationships by scheduling time for regular get-togethers."

And more pointedly, "The people you love deserve more than getting whatever time is left over. If someone is important to you, make regular time for them on your calendar."

46

TAKE YOUR TIME
WITH THE PRESENT.

How you spend your time determines how you live your life.

Mae Jemison was busy in college. She majored in chemical engineering and African and Afro-American studies, led the Black Student Union, and directed a musical production. She later earned many titles: doctor, astronaut, professor, and founder.

Her approach to time: "There are 86,400 seconds in each day, and each one of those seconds is extremely precious because we can choose to do with each one of those seconds exactly as we please, but we can never get a single one of those seconds back."

And balance: "We have to be able to party enough so that we can get a smile, but not that we get tired. And we have to be able to work hard enough that we might be a little tired, but we don't lose our smile."

Psychologist Phil Zimbardo stresses that people daily face choices involving a range of times. With John Boyd, he writes, "By opening your mind fully to the present moment, you give up longing and desire for future possibilities and surrender past regrets and obligations."

Zimbardo and Boyd point out you have three different ways to combine time and happiness. You can "reexperience past happiness whenever you remember it. . . . Immerse yourself in happiness and pleasure in the present. . . . [And] plan to be happy in the future and to derive pleasure from the expectation of future happiness."

They describe time as a gift, to be shared with friends through walks, conversations, and dinners. They also note that it is a gift you should give yourself through "downtime, play time, fun time, exercise time, indulgence time." And for balance, "Try to reserve at least one weekend day as a workless day."

47

DO NOTHING.

Not To-Do List
1. Binge watching
2. Doomscrolling
3. Web surfing

Before you start, you need to stop.

That's advice from business school professor Chip Heath and his brother Dan, who study how we make decisions. They note people often don't take time to define their most important priorities. If you do ask managers what their core priorities are, these rarely match up with what they devoted time to in the previous week.

To get to what matters, you need to identify what doesn't. The Heaths recommend creating a "stop-doing list." That clears away time for you to pursue what is important.

Putting the list to use requires conscious action. As the Heaths recommend, "Make it concrete: Look back over your schedule for the past week and ask yourself, *What, specifically would I have given up to carve out the extra three or four or five hours that I'll need?*"

Teaching digital art, Jenny Odell encountered students stressed by pursuit of achievement and glued to their screens. She saw this as part of a broader market-driven ecosystem, "where every waking moment has become the time in which we make our living, and when we submit even our leisure for numerical evaluation via likes on Facebook and Instagram, constantly checking on its performance like one checks a stock."

Eventually she wrote a book entitled *How to Do Nothing*, a surprising title from a university instructor. *Nothing* here does not mean "inaction." Rather, "the first half of 'doing nothing' is about disengaging from the attention economy; the other half is about reengaging with something else."

That something else involves putting your phone down and shifting attention to people and places. It could be spending time in nature. Or it might lead to "true conviviality—the dinners and gatherings and celebrations that give us the emotional sustenance we need."

48

EAT, SLEEP, EXERCISE.

You can't go up if you're run down.

Dr. Emma Seppala, science director of the Center for Compassion and Altruism Research and Education, says that "most of us are not kind to ourselves in our quest for success."

She says that in rushing through days and working into the night, "we try to compensate for the stress we feel with habits that harm our health. We eat the wrong foods, drink, stay up too late, and forget to exercise—or we overexercise."

Working too hard stifles creativity. Professor Myron Scholes won the Nobel Prize in Economics for theoretical work about stock options. Describing how he finds new ideas, Scholes talks about taking walks, golfing, and meditating. Getting away from distractions yields insights, for as Scholes told Seppala, "It gives you the ability to see other perspectives, let ideas percolate, challenge your views, gather additional data."

Kelly McGonigal studies health psychology, lectures at a university, and teaches dance and group exercise. For the author of *The Joy of Movement*, those three activities are deeply related.

She notes, "From dance, I had learned that no matter how worried and discouraged I felt at the beginning of class, the music and movement would transport me to a state of optimism. And from my toughest cardio workouts, I had learned that a pounding heart is not always a sign of fear. Sometimes, it is proof that your heart is being strengthened."

Exercising leads to happiness and connection via joy, for McGonigal observes, "Joy is what ties together the neurochemistry of the runner's high, the elation of moving in synchrony, and the unity sensation in nature. It's what draws us to ritual and music, and what makes achieving a personal best, cooperating with others, and witnessing someone else's triumph so satisfying."

49

GOING TO EXTREMES IS NOT AN ACHIEVEMENT.

ZZZZ
ZZZ
Z
Z
Z
Z
Z
zZZZZ

There are no medals in the stress Olympics.

Betsy Kim got a lot done on campus: majored in economics, cofounded a club called the Asian Women's Alliance with her friends, served as a French conversation partner, and wrote humor pieces for the newspaper. She also took time to relax.

But around her, she saw peers working to extremes. She said, "It's tempting to believe that if you sacrifice essential/non-negotiable elements of your health and well-being to fit one more thing into your day—or that if you feel awful because you haven't slept, you must be doing something right."

Kim knew the opposite was true: "Less is more—you'll be able to live a life that is more productive and better aligned with your values when you're well-rested, well-fed, and spending time with loved ones etc., not when you're chugging a Red Bull to stay awake because you took 24 units!"

Melissa A. Hosek teaches first-year students and knows why they're tired.

She says, "I see many students neglect their sleep. Sometimes, it is because they are busy with homework. Other times, it is because they are not managing their socializing time well. Regardless, poor sleep fuels a vicious cycle of stress, which students may not realize until it is too late."

Her advice to lagging students is simple and easy to follow: "Go to sleep in the same day that you woke up in. . . . If you wake up on Tuesday, you should go to sleep before Wednesday."

She also points out that learning is challenging: "I see students who sheepishly confess 'I don't understand,' 'I'm not very good at this,' or 'this is hard.' That is perfectly fine! If you already knew the material perfectly, then you would not need to come to college in the first place. This is a time to learn, grow, and make mistakes."

REFLECTION–
ESTABLISH PRIORITIES.

It's possible to get all As and flunk life.

When I read that insight from novelist Walker Percy in college, I was uneasy. What if life were like a course? I knew I wasn't formally enrolled, definitely lacked the syllabus, and had no clue about the midterm and the final.

As a student and later as a professor, I valued As. You earn them if you work hard to answer questions posed by others. They represent a standard of excellence and signal you're developing critical thinking skills.

They're a narrow definition of success, though. In life *you* have to define the questions that are important to answer and search without a predefined set of readings and assignments. Earning As in courses may lead to a remunerative day job. That leaves wide-open questions about what type of work is satisfying and how and with whom to spend your nights and weekends.

My favorite teacher in college gave one lecture on Percy, but that day sparked a lifelong interest. I've read Percy's novels, essays, biographies, and family histories. On trips to New Orleans, I scout scenes from his work. I have traveled to his gravesite, whose simplicity reflects his faith and humility.

In my twenties, I would give new friends a copy of Percy's novel *The Moviegoer*, whose protagonist's search for meaning and love resonates with me. A close friend reached out to Percy to have him autograph a book for me (a volume titled, ironically, *Lost in the Cosmos: The Last Self-Help Book*). When I reread his novels now, the differences in what I see and value teach me about how I've changed over time.

This isn't an infomercial for Walker Percy. His works comment on a rapidly changing popular culture, so references can appear dated or elusive. It is a pitch, though, for you to undertake your own search for guides to what matters, both inside and outside the classroom.

When you're in class, be there. The temptation in a lecture class is to treat the professor like a TV. You may surf, shop, text, and circle back to see what's going on with a slide or class discussion. Multitasking may give you a sense of accomplishment, but you run the risk of missing what's important but not on the test. You can't predict when a comment or question will spark an important insight for you, but you can raise the odds of missing it if your mind is online rather than focused on the discussion.

Once you're outside the classroom, be outside. Fill your calendar with your own assignments: time with friends, walks or runs, and sleep. Be present in these moments, which may mean turning off the phone or leaving devices in another room. If you let likes and alerts and algorithms run your day, advertisers will be happy, but you won't be.

It's good to know deadlines for class assignments and job applications. It's also important to set your own goals for how you spend your time. College inevitably involves stress, sadness, and times of loneliness. Taking advantage of counseling services on campus is a way to navigate those challenges.

You can also make your college life easier if you share it with others. Going to a movie, turning out to watch or join a game, and even shopping for a party can get you outside of yourself and focused on others.

You will someday have the college degree, T-shirt, and coffee mug. The memories that make you smile and conversations that make you thankful, however, will come from the people you made time to get to know.

CONNECTING

50

YOUR FRIENDS WILL SHOW UP IN YOUR HIGHLIGHT REEL.

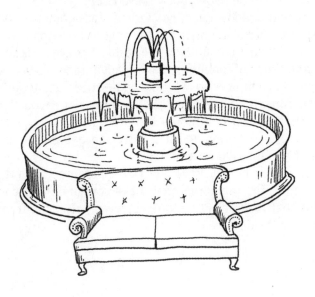

You don't just go to college. You are college for someone, and they're college for you.

As a senior, Emma Coleman observed, education seems solitary, "but behind each one of us are hundreds of people who have helped along our paths. Like your freshman roommate who worked with you on your psets until 3 a.m. The TA who wrote your recommendation even though you asked four hours before the deadline. The stranger who warned you that the chicken at Arrillaga was extra-dry that day. All these people offered help so generously, asking for nothing in return."

Coleman notes friends make education possible: "Stanford is all the acts of kindness along the way. . . . Stanford is those who were there when you were lost. They helped you whether you had the courage and the strength to ask for help or not."

In his senior column for the campus newspaper, sportswriter Bobby Pragada encouraged classmates to remember an anecdote of their own: "A poetry reading, the fifth time you saw 'Avengers: Endgame,' an a cappella concert, a rally in White Plaza, a cool bird you saw by Lake Lag, Ryan Burns' 70 yard comeback drive against UCLA. . . . Think about how special that anecdote is to you, and how you felt when you experienced it."

He then pulls back the camera to reveal more about that treasured time: "I'm willing to bet that there was at least one person right next to you, a person you shared that experience with, who has brought as much joy—if not more—into your life, who enhanced that moment beyond just what it truly was. Sports (much like life) are always better when there's someone you love cheering alongside you."

51

CREATE TIME FOR IMPORTANT RELATIONSHIPS.

Classes have start times. So do friendships.

For distance runner Lauren Fleshman, that was Sunday mornings. She says, "The anchor of my personal college sports experience became the Sunday long run, where I fell more and more deeply in love with running—and Jesse Thomas along with it.... We'd unfold our cramped bodies and open our strides, forgetting what any of this training was for besides play after a mile or two."

They eventually fell for each other, then broke up. She says, "We were on and off romantically, but we always had our Sunday long run." The time became a haven. Fleshman remembers, "Those runs were the reset button I looked forward to after every competition."

There were many meets for Fleshman, who won five NCAA championships. And on a Sunday four years after graduating, she married her longtime running partner, Jesse Thomas.

Business school professor Cassie Holmes studies happiness for a living.

Her takeaway: "The single biggest predictor of greater overall satisfaction in life is having strong and supportive relationships (family, or friends that feel like family)." She also warns, "Regrets of inaction (i.e., not doing something you wish you had) sneak up and stick around to form the greatest of life regrets. So go ahead and act now to avoid any major regrets later."

When she interviewed people about happiness, extraordinary experiences cited included "going to a concert, attending a professional sporting event, eating at a world-renowned restaurant."

Ordinary moments of bliss included a "simple moment shared with a loved one (including pets)—getting a text from a friend, a good-morning kiss ... lounging with one's dog."

What these moments share is intention, a decision to take time to spend connecting with people. Without that commitment, life crowds out friendships.

52

BE OPEN TO LOVE.

To greet you need to meet.

The first week of college is a whirl, but Susan Rice made time to go to her dorm's ice-cream social. There she met Ian Cameron, a senior from British Columbia—which caused Rice to ask, "Is that in South America?"

A few days later they met again at a football game and ended up jumping into a fountain with the Stanford Band. On Halloween he sent her a dozen roses. In November Rice called her mother to say, "I met this guy. He's wickedly funny and extremely nice. It might be starting to become something."

Cameron graduated and eventually returned to Canada to work. Rice notes they ultimately agreed, "While we were living apart, we would remain a couple but could also date other people if we wanted." Almost ten years after the ice-cream social, they (very happily) married.

Falling in love in college normally does not lead to marriage, and Mae Jemison argues that's a good thing. She notes, "At that stage in life, very few people actually know what they want. Those who believe they do, often want something or someone that may not be right or beneficial for them. You are still learning not only about the world but also about yourself at a very fast pace; with any luck you will continue to learn things about yourself, your career, your likes and dislikes."

Jemison brings multiple perspectives to this analysis: alum, doctor, professor, and astronaut (the ultimate long view). She notes, "More likely than not, that boy or girl will not be the love of your life. . . . Boyfriends and girlfriends always, always seem to mess up in some way close to finals or important midterms. They're not malicious, it's probably just the stress."

53

DON'T FLAKE ON YOUR FRIENDS.

Friendship is an opportunity that comes with a cost.

As an econ major, Betsy Kim knew trade-offs were important. Time with friends meant time away from studying. Yet Kim came to realize this in college: "How beautiful and foundational friendships in my life could be if I tended to them."

Supporting someone is easy to define: "Be there for the important moments in your friends' lives, and celebrate their achievements."

Going to a birthday party—or better yet, organizing one—can celebrate a friend. Something will often come up that tempts you to skip the event. Kim advises against flaking, "because your friends and their time are not an infinite resource."

She notes, "The friends who make time for you during the busiest times in college (midterms, finals, etc.) are generally the ones you'll stay in touch with after graduation as well."

Time with friends comes in many different sizes.

As one senior put it, "Big parties are a lot of fun, and when I've been super busy I've sometimes saved my only social time for big parties where I know I could see all of my friends." He learned, though, that "parties aren't often the best time to hear how people are doing, what they're up to, difficulties they might be having. The music is loud, energy is high, and it's really fun, but the connection isn't that deep."

He contrasted that with small moments: "A lunch with a friend, an evening walk, late night videogames, or food runs. These moments are where I've found the most meaningful connections happen."

Describing the week before graduation, he said, "When we realized that we might not see each other for a really long time we didn't all focus on partying together, all we wanted was more small moments."

54

DRINKS ARE ON YOU.

Mantras take many forms.

In a commencement address, Issa Rae shared that hers is a song lyric: "I pull up at the club VIP, gas tank on E, but all dranks on ME. Wipe Me Down."

Deconstructing the song, she said you should show up at the club of life "as someone who belongs and deserves to be here." And "no matter what obstacles or dire circumstances you personally face, you should always value and celebrate your community."

Struggling to develop the series *The Misadventures of Awkward Black Girl*, Rae had friends from school step up to act, write, produce, and fund. She said, "They rallied together to 'buy drinks' and help me make the series."

Rae notes that as you face questions after college, answers may come from people who have been "sitting right next to you, or across from you, or behind you."

Samantha Wong started her life as a college journalist with a rejection from her college newspaper.

That disappointment led to possibilities. Wong said, "Each rejection and failure I have received over the years (and I have received many) stung, but they forced me to carve new identities."

Wong learned what she could control was showing up for others: "I could be caring, I realize, when I wrap upset friends in hugs or listen to a resident update me on their life. I could be witty, I notice, when I write the perfect pun for a teaser headline or crack a joke that makes my friends literally roll with laughter."

Eventually she became the paper's executive editor, noting in her final column, "I hope I remember what it's like to be 21 and my truest self, someone who is not just unafraid of, but craves, sincerity and rawness in every experience."

55

THE NETWORK
CAN GET YOU WORK.

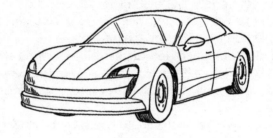

Your friends may someday be your colleagues.

Guy Kawasaki and Mike Boich met as sophomores "and hit it off immediately because of a shared love of cars." A decade later, Boich hired Kawasaki at Apple.

Kawasaki admits, "I got the job through nepotism—the practice of people giving jobs to their friends and relatives." But he notes, "The day after you start a job, nobody cares about your connections, history, and credentials—or lack thereof. You either deliver results, or you don't."

Kawasaki says he thrived for a simple reason: "I loved to work. There are people who are smarter than me. There are people who work harder than me. But there are few people who are both."

His advice: "Get in at any level you can. . . . The level you rise to is what's important, not the level at which you entered."

As seniors, Susan Rice and Mike McFaul worked to convince their school to stop holding "stocks in companies that invested in apartheid South Africa." Both went to Oxford as Rhodes Scholars and earned PhDs in international relations.

Thirty years later, Rice reached out to invite McFaul to become an advisor on Senator Barack Obama's fledgling presidential campaign. McFaul says as he pondered the offer, "She told me to 'get my shit together' and join this historic ride."

Though McFaul did not know Obama's foreign policy positions, he said, "Susan was on board and that was enough for me. I had no idea that saying yes out of loyalty to a friend that day would alter my professional life for the next seven years."

Under President Obama, Rice served as US ambassador to the United Nations, then as national security advisor. McFaul joined the National Security Council and later became US ambassador to Russia.

56

WEAK TIES ARE STRONG.

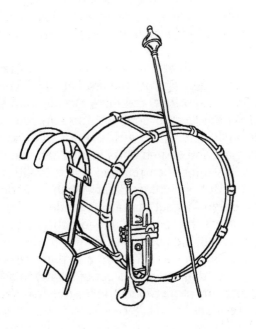

Sometimes it's who you moderately know.

Sociologist Mark Granovetter found that acquaintances, people you have infrequent and less intense contact with, can be more helpful than close friends and family when you're searching for work. They're more likely to travel in different networks, which means they may learn about jobs and opportunities you don't know about. Granovetter called this phenomenon "The Strength of Weak Ties."

Economist Erik Brynjolfsson and coauthors set out to test the theory on LinkedIn. Over five years, twenty million users were randomly connected with people they had weak or strong ties with. Sometimes these connections led them to learn about new opportunities and to switch jobs. The researchers found the most increase in job mobility came from people you have moderately weak ties with.

Brynjolfsson also discovered that "adding weak ties creates significantly more labor market mobility in digital and high-tech sectors."

And that helps explain how American studies major Elise Grangaard ended up working at a Wi-Fi systems start-up.

Grangaard had played trumpet in the school marching band. Three years after graduating, she reconnected with the drum major from the band for dinner. They had gotten "to know each other well, on a Band road trip to Texas, leaving at midnight and not stopping until the next night. The long conversations in the car were their bonding moment."

Catching up at a Sunday night dinner, she learned from her friend that the start-up where he worked would soon be hiring. Tuesday she applied, Thursday she interviewed, and Monday she had a job offer, which she accepted.

The moral—she "found her job not from closest friends, and not from posted job notices, but from someone who would seem unlikely to be helpful: a friend she hadn't seen in a while."

57
EXTRAS CAN
BE ESSENTIAL.

"It won't be the whole of your Stanford experience. But it just might end up being the best and brightest part."

Erin Woo wrote those words about writing for the campus newspaper. But they apply broadly to college extracurriculars, a source of friendships, leadership experience, and life lessons.

In her senior column, Woo recounted these memories: "Late production nights eating pizza and tossing around banter as we blew past print deadlines time and time again. Breaking news stories at any hour of the day or night, dropping everything to jump on my bike and race to the Daily house, all of us crowded around one speakerphone, six people tripping over each other on the same Google doc."

As editor-in-chief, she learned the challenges of leadership: "The weight of being the final call on every decision. The responsibility of running this organization, a duct-taped miracle of moving parts."

For Hannah Knowles, as for Woo, the newspaper was a training ground for becoming a professional journalist.

Covering the university taught Knowles the essentials of reporting. Describing life at a college newspaper, she observed, "You'll talk to some people you disagree with, with the goal of understanding their view. You'll dig into nuance, finding all sorts of beliefs challenged in the face of another person's concrete experience."

Extracurriculars also teach you about yourself. Knowles says about reporting for the campus paper, "You'll encounter pushy people and figure out, over time, how to hold your ground. . . . You'll become a more curious person, empowered when you have questions to go talk to people who can help you find the answers. You'll learn to be persistent: to make that extra phone call, send the follow-up email or show up unannounced."

After graduation, Knowles joined the *Washington Post*, where she eventually became a national politics reporter.

58

TO GO FAR,
GO TOGETHER.

Cory Booker often cites this proverb about connecting. As a frosh at Stanford, he got to live it.

Flying back to school, Booker thought he had two empty seats as companions. Suddenly he heard screams, and a mother with a baby and little boy appeared.

The nineteen-year-old Booker realized, "I could accept this now as being the worst flight of my life or I can make it different.... I decided that I was going to make this the best flight of my life. I started telling this little boy jokes and he started laughing at my horrible jokes.... Like, why, what do you call your mother's sister who runs away and gets married? An Antelope." Happiness ensued on board.

Fifteen years later the mother recognized Booker as he ran for Newark mayor. Her son volunteered, and she became a campaign donor.

When the rapper Jidenna was an undergraduate, he started a social group called Fear & Fancy, which fostered musical collaborations and put on events such as a "massQuerade ball." He reached out to an up-and-coming singer named Janelle Monáe to perform at a function, and she agreed.

Jidenna went on to have a hit entitled "Classic Man." As his agent encouraged him to tour with stars, Jidenna instead chose Stromae, a Belgian singer relatively unknown in the United States because he sang in French.

Janelle Monáe went on to found Wondaland Records, which signed Jidenna. Stromae went on to sell out Madison Square Garden, with Janelle Monáe and Jidenna as openers.

Citing the Kenyan saying "You are your friends," Jidenna observed, "By letting Stromae and Monae into my world and them letting me in, I picked up how to become a fashionable yet absurd artist ... in the best way possible."

59
GO GLOBAL.

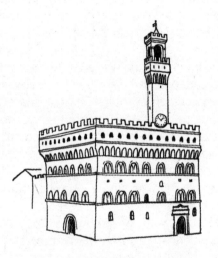

Going abroad, you learn about the world—and yourself.

Amanda Rizkalla came to college as a first-generation, low-income student excited about exploring with the support of financial aid.

Her first stop was Italy: "I spent winter quarter of my junior year in Florence, where I took classes in film studies, Italian language, abstract art and contemporary Italian politics and culture, in addition to working as a culinary intern at a restaurant near the palace (yes, palace) where classes are held." She spent the next quarter at Oxford.

Reflecting, she says, "I learned how to get by in a country whose primary language I did not speak fluently. I learned how to navigate two different cultures and what it meant to approach them as an American. I learned how to ask for help when I needed it—from program staff, from new friends and even from strangers."

Commencement day is bittersweet. But Richard Engel told graduating seniors to view the day as a beginning, saying, "You are about to start your adventures."

He urged them to consider moving abroad, noting, "This is the time in your lives to gamble. You are all here today because of years of hard work and discipline.... Breaking rocks is hard work too. So is a Stairmaster, but it doesn't get you anywhere. This is the time to make a big bet and see if it pays off."

Engel's bet was moving to Cairo, which led to life as a foreign correspondent. Describing the uncertainty of landing in a new country, he said, "Put yourself in situations where you don't know what's going on around you and let your brain sort it out. That's the fun part: the constant learning, the new sensations, the new place and the new risks."

60
GO TO OFFICE HOURS.

Email killed office hours.

When I started teaching, students would come by office hours to talk about ideas, current events, and graduate school. I'd ask about their plans for summer internships or future careers. I also found myself sharing insights into navigating college, such as, "No existential thoughts during exam period. . . . It's possible to get all As and flunk life. . . . Life is more essay than short answer."

Email stopped these conversations. Instead of coming by in person, students sent very specific questions about paper extensions and class content. A note I received from a former student I often talked with shows what's been lost. Reflecting on how she'd just used in her current work ideas we'd discussed nearly three decades ago, she wrote, "I am really going to give you credit for having somehow implanted deceptively influential knowledge deep in my 18 yr old brain."

Office hours can be a place to find mentors, who can end up being friends for life.

Jim Tankersley arrived on campus "as a scared freshman with way too much confidence in my writing abilities." He got into William Woo's Writing and Reporting the News class, which shaped Tankersley's college experience and future career. In the course, he said, "[Woo] ran us through mock news events and forced us to write on deadline. To imbue us with journalistic ethics, he unspooled hours-long, perfectly crafted tales of his news-gathering youth."

Woo became a mentor and friend for Tankersley, currently an economic policy correspondent at the *New York Times*. Speaking at Woo's funeral, Tankersley noted that he kept the papers from Woo's class because of their insightful margin notes, such as this one: "I really hope you keep this message with you always. . . . There are no quick fixes, ever, for the things we hold dearest."

61

ASK FOR HELP.

Asking is about giving and getting.

Your questions give someone a chance to help, and you get the opportunity to learn.

When Hakeem Oluseyi was struggling in a physics PhD program, he turned to a classmate named Daveed because they "both felt like outsiders." Oluseyi explained, "I trusted him enough to ask him any question, because I knew he was never going to look down on me."

The methods could be unorthodox. Oluseyi says, "Using beer mugs, coasters, and saltshakers as props, Daveed could illustrate obscure theories of particle or quantum physics I'd struggled for hours to learn from a textbook."

The more they talked, the more confident Oluseyi grew. He came to appreciate Daveed's advice on charting your own course: "There are a thousand ways to understand a physics problem and a thousand different paths to the right solution. You just have to find your best path."

Student journeys increasingly involve taking advantage of mental health counseling and wellness programs.

One administrator notes, "The common narrative among students was, 'I'm capable and competent. I can't let anyone know I am struggling.' That narrative has changed. Now, many students *are* asking for help."

Counseling helps when, as one junior put it, you are "sad, or distressed, or scared, or feeling unstable." Talking about mental illness, he said, "It is a chronic condition, and I've settled into a rhythm of reluctant acceptance that allows me to continue my life plans in relative peace."

He went on to advise friends, "Instead of telling me that you don't know how to help me, just tell me you're listening. That you heard what I said—that I'm feeling stressed about my classes, that my crush didn't work out, that I have to reshuffle my schedule for the umpteenth time. . . . Just listen."

62

ASK ABOUT HOME.

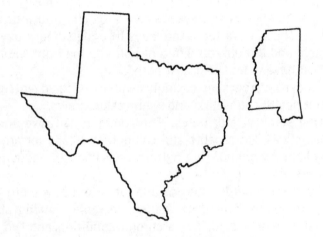

Home can be the place you're from—or returning to.

Describing her high school years in Texas, Lenora Chu says, "I was programmed as tightly as a cable box with a thousand channels: Advanced Placement classes, Academic Decathlon, SAT summer prep, Sunday Chinese school." Expectations for her were clear: "Grades should be perfect, dating ignored until college, and dance class and sports strictly elective."

There were battles at home. Chu recalls, "In my last few years at home, my father and I fought viciously over the right to direct my future. . . . Ours was a classic story of Chinese expectations meets American culture and a strong-willed personality."

While Chu majored in engineering in college, she ended up covering the world as a journalist. She now lives in Berlin and reports on Europe as an international correspondent for the *Christian Science Monitor*.

When Jesmyn Ward came to school in California, part of her stayed in Mississippi.

She says, "I would beg long conversations on the phone with my friends at home so I could listen to the sounds in the background, wishing I were there. . . . I knew there was much to hate about home, the racism and the inequality and the poverty, which is why I'd left, yet I loved it."

Graduating with a BA in English and an MA in communication, Ward returned home, only to leave again in search of work. She described herself as "yearning to leave the South and doing so again and again, but perpetually called back to home by a love so thick it choked me."

Ward eventually settled in Mississippi, writing novels recognized with a MacArthur genius award for "exploring the enduring bonds of community and familial love among poor African Americans of the rural South."

63

ASK QUESTIONS.

That's advice Dr. Atul Gawande gives medical students learning to interact with patients. But it applies more broadly.

Gawande notes the query could be simple: "'Where did you grow up?' Or: 'What made you move to Boston?' Even: 'Did you watch last night's Red Sox game?' You don't have to come up with a deep or important question, just one that lets you make a human connection."

As a surgeon who's also a writer, Gawande approaches interactions with strangers as a chance to learn. The conversation might start with a patient, medical assistant, or nurse. The questions and the answers make roles and organizations feel "less like a machine."

Gawande says, "It's not that making this connection necessarily helps anyone. But you start to remember the people you see, instead of letting them all blur together. And sometimes you discover the unexpected."

Questions come naturally to Joe Dworetzky, a lawyer who went back to school to get a journalism degree.

He saw students living away from home for the first time struggle with challenges: "Relationships, peer conflicts, money, time management, difficult professors, not getting into a chosen fraternity or sorority, keeping up with brilliant peers." The sharing of highly curated lives on social media added to these pressures.

Dworetzky knew the pathway forward in college involved asking for help. He said, "Universities have so many people who could give help if they were asked. From RA's to full professors to college deans, there are people who are caring, knowledgeable and want to engage but the student needs to lead."

There are people on campus rooting for your success and ready to answer questions. As Dworetzky says, "All the social problems have been seen before by someone, the mission is to tap into those who have."

REFLECTION– MAKE TIME FOR FRIENDS.

Your future friends won't knock on your door. You need to seek them out.

The people you meet in college can be friends for life. You'll make and share memories centered around meals, games, classes, parties, romances, breakups, summers, and work. Late-night conversations with classmates, often supplemented by a food run, are a way to make sense of your day. Yet how do you find the people who will end up in your college highlight reel?

Start conversations. I met my best friend in college while standing in line the first week of school. He asked me to inscribe his "Facebook," a directory with student names and pictures, with the memories we'd be sharing over the next four years. Those ended up including days spent organizing political events, nights running loops around campus libraries, double dates to a waltz, and many games of Twister. Memories I couldn't foresee included going to each other's weddings, hiking with our wives and sons, and looking back on decades of friendship at reunion events.

Embrace serendipity. The most impactful event I went to in college was a panel discussion about midterm elections. I don't remember the analysis, but a chance conversation with an audience member led to hot chocolate at a diner. Discovery of shared interests (politics) and differences (about art and music) led to friendship. I almost missed out on this mean-ingful relationship because the night was cold and staying in looked preferable. I rallied, went to the panel, and ended up in a conversation and friendship that spanned several years.

Treat meals like real breaks. You'll see people at parties, but you'll really get to know them by sharing food, time, and ideas. Eating on the run can appear efficient. Yet when seniors rank where they learned the most in college, they often place friends at number one, followed by extracurriculars. The bronze goes to professors and classes, though you could argue that discussions with friends are often sparked by classes. Ultimately, taking time to schedule meals with friends is as important to your education as going to sections.

Find mentors. Most professors could earn more if they left academia. Many choose to stay because they like teaching. Office hours are your chance to meet these mentors. You can raise questions about the discipline, ask what drew a professor to research, or seek out career advice. You may even end up working as their research assistant. Connecting with a professor around substantive work makes school more enlightening and enjoyable.

Trust the process. My first week in college I heard many times that somewhere on campus were my friends for life. At the end of that week, I went to a dance in a hall cavernous enough to fit the entire class. The music was loud, people were exuberant, and I was lost. I walked outside, stared at the sky, and wondered if this was going to be my college life.

Four decades later, I was in that same hall with those same classmates. The music was loud, people were exuberant, and I was too. Friends I'd made across four years were sharing memories of music, politics, and families. Classmates I text with every day were there in person, sharing real smiles rather than emojis. And I was dancing with my soulmate. We met eight years after graduation, but the experiences I'd had as an undergraduate had prepared me to recognize her.

If you treat finding and nurturing friendships like a highly important class, it will make your life a continuing education.

IDENTITY

64
EMBRACE DIVERSITY.

Who speaks for the trees?

The Lorax, of course. But who speaks for the tree cutters?

Since he came from Oregon's timber country, Jim Tankersley offered a different perspective on forests to his college classmates. He said, "I grew up understanding that those trees weren't just yuletide decorations or some sort of museum collection for Portlanders to admire. . . . They gave jobs to our neighbors."

The decline of logging decimated opportunities for his high school classmates and set Tankersley on a quest as a journalist to understand economic inequality.

He found that a significant source of growth since 1960 came from reducing discrimination. As he put it, "Expanding opportunity for women and minority workers kept the economy growing fast enough to generate the wage gains that lifted all those workers, male and female, white and black and otherwise, into the middle class." A diverse workforce was good business.

Not everyone sees value in difference.

Poet Molly McCully Brown navigated college in a wheelchair because of cerebral palsy. She knows this leads people to see her differently.

Brown describes putting off "sending the email in which I have to write and tell the woman interviewing me for a job on Tuesday that I'm in a wheelchair. I worry about the mother who emailed me about tutoring her daughter in SAT prep, and then just stopped writing after I revealed I use one."

Though strangers view her as disabled, Brown notes what she's learned from life marked by physical constraints: "It gave me empathy and maturity. It gave me discipline and poetry, and enough hurt and strangeness to really need it. And I wouldn't trade away anything that might take with it the way I fill up when I read Emily Dickinson. *After great pain, a formal feeling comes.*"

65
EMBRACE
COMMON HUMANITY.

The struggle is real, but it's also shared.

When you face a challenge in college, it is sometimes hard to determine the source. Is it you? The way people react to your identity? Your school? College life in general?

Psychologist Claude Steele and colleagues saw that racial segregation in friendship networks meant that students failed to see their common challenges. When they brought students of different races together in a dorm to talk late at night over pizza, that changed.

The conversations "revealed that the stresses of college life—a lower test grade than expected, an unreturned telephone call to a teaching assistant or classmate, an unfriendly interaction with another student, a chronic shortage of cash, and so on—happen to everyone regardless of race."

That insight was particularly liberating for Black students participating in the discussions. It reduced their concerns and gave them more freedom to learn.

Our bodies are a common denominator and connection for people.

As a junior, Kory Gaines went to see a performance by the Alvin Ailey American Dance Theater, famous for its fusion of African American heritage and modern dance.

Ailey once said, "I am trying to show the world that we are all human beings." Gaines came away with that appreciation. He concluded that performance creates a sense of connection among "the dancer, the musician, the choreographer, the artists, the mass crowd, the students and the teacher."

The performance was meaningful and memorable for Gaines, who said, "I remember the beat of my heart, the rush of my blood. . . . I felt alive, human. I felt this way because people, groups of people, embraced and worked together at their talents."

Gaines appreciated both the dancers' community and their creativity, noting, "I find comfort knowing our bodies can communicate and speculate, imagine and intuit."

66
CATEGORIES ARE MIXED AND SOMETIMES FRACTURED.

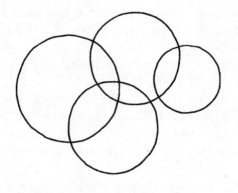

What are you?

With a Japanese mother and Irish American father, Stephen Murphy-Shigematsu gets that question a lot. The short answer is many things.

Murphy-Shigematsu embraces multiple identities, choosing "to live in borderlands of nations and races." He notes, "I am a Japanese who is also American; I am Westerner and Easterner; I am a man who takes care of kids; I am a Catholic who is Buddhist. I identify with all these groups, not confining myself to any."

In Japan and in America, he's often seen as a foreigner. That sense of separation and distancing, though, makes him more empathetic and less likely to "see the world as Us versus Them."

His approach is more about bonding than boundaries: "I try to see the Other in myself and myself in the Other. I try to be human and regard others as human."

For Vicki L. Ruiz, her scholarship focused on race, class, and gender began at the kitchen table.

Ruiz says, "[As] a child, I learned two types of history—the one at home and the one at school." Her mother and grandmother told her "stories of village life, coal mines, strikes, discrimination, and family lore." Those accounts were missing from textbooks.

When Ruiz went on to get a history PhD, she found that in scholarship about Mexican Americans, the "reader has a vague awareness of the presence of women, but only as scenery, not as actors . . . and even their celebrated maternal roles are sketched in muted shades."

She filled this gap by writing *From Out of the Shadows*, which chronicles Mexican American "women's border journeys not solely in terms of travel, but of internal migration—creating, accommodating, resisting, and transforming the physical and psychological environs of their 'new' lives in the United States."

67

IDENTITY CAN TAKE A TOLL.

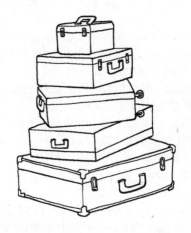

Your real audience is one—you.

Lenora Chu's parents both immigrated to America. For her this meant she "grew up under the invisible hand of ancestral expectation, which clutched my shoulder with the intensity of a vise grip."

At home her parents "wielded their authority without mercy, plotting mine and my sister's paths to test perfection and advanced degrees." Her achievements were met not with praise but with the question "What's next?" When she got into her dream school, her father said, "You better be worth it."

Chu notes, "A little praise heaped on my childhood shoulders might have helped quiet some demons, the ones with sharp, haunting voices that many of my Chinese and Chinese American friends speak of. These little guys cling to your collarbone and whisper . . . 'You're not good enough, you're not doing enough, someone's always doing more, and doing better.'"

Identities sometimes come with baggage that you don't want to carry.

We all face situations where it's easier to self-censor rather than express an unpopular viewpoint. As Lily Zheng and Inge Hansen put it, people "can find themselves torn between their loyalty to their community and the freedom and opportunities that come with doing what it takes to get ahead, whether that means distancing from an identity, hiding it, or even using it for profit."

They note pressure to live up to ideals is punishing, since "the perfect woman or Black person or queer or trans or disabled or fill-in-the-blank person does not exist."

Their recommended manifesto: "Whatever my identities, beliefs, or values are, I get to determine for myself how to hold them and express myself to the world. I get to determine whether I want more safety, comfort, or well-being at any point and to own those desires."

68
WRITE YOUR OWN STORY.

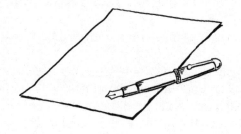

Self-doubt has many sources.

Those include categories people may define you by, such as gender and age.

A poet who returned to graduate school in her fifties to study literature recalls the awkward reception she received from some students and professors. She recounts, "I could see the dismissive looks, the mocking sideways glances, the disinterested turns of head." She realized the insidious toll this treatment was taking on her confidence.

Her advice to those similarly battling externally imposed definitions:

1. Be aware. Notice your thoughts. As painful as they may be, better to see them clearly. Then, you can see the point of choice. You can decide how to handle them. You can notice that it's not necessary to believe them, it's not necessary to pick them up. Easier said than done, but practice over time can help re-write the soundtrack.

2. Counter-narrative. Everything you are afraid people are thinking—write it down, all of it. Now, write down what you *know* to be true—based on your own experience of who you know yourself to be, from the time before college or grad school. Write down all your successes, any time you've felt any sense of confidence, however small. From this place of knowing, write a counter statement to each of the menu items above. They can be affirmations, they can be lines from a poem, they can be come-backs, they can be snippets of advice from trusted ones. Write them down. And have them handy when the fears crop up, as they will.

3. Write down the name of one person who believes in you or one person who inspires you. Write down their words. Bring them to mind when you need to. Even just conjuring an image of the person's face or voice can be calming or centering.

69

DON'T REACT
TO EVERYTHING.

You do you.

Condoleezza Rice has had many powerful positions: professor, provost, national security advisor, secretary of state.

As a Black woman, she's faced discrimination. She notes that "race is a constant factor in American life." She argues that what's important is how you deal with this reality, since "reacting to every incident, real or imagined, is crippling, tiring, and ultimately counterproductive."

Rice traces her resilience to her parents. She says, "I'd grown up in a family that believed you might not control your circumstances but you could control your reaction to them. There was no room for being a victim."

She's an optimist: "Despite the gross inequities my ancestors faced, there *has* been progress, and race is no longer determinative of how far one can go."

And a realist: "America is not color-blind and likely will never be."

Issa Rae's memoir is entitled *The Misadventures of Awkward Black Girl*. In the book, she writes, "I love being black. . . . The problem is that I don't want to always *talk* about it because honestly, talking about being 'black' is extremely tiring."

She says race can be central: "Sometimes, I'm so deep in my anger, my irritation, my need to stir change, that I can't see anything outside of the lens of race."

Other days, she sets it aside and argues, "*Isn't this what those who came before me fought for?* The right *not* to have to deal with race?"

Rae says, "For the majority of my life I cared too much about how my blackness was perceived." She landed on a different approach, "to focus only on the positivity of being black, and especially of being a black woman."

People might disagree with this approach, but she asks, "Who is to say what we do and don't do? What we can and can't do?"

70

YOU CAN COUNTER STEREOTYPE THREATS.

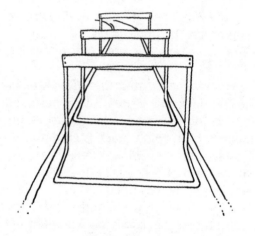

You may know your story, but telling it can be hard.

As a five-time NCAA running champion, Lauren Fleshman was psyched to be the face of a Nike campaign for a new shoe "designed around modern biomechanical research on the female body." But when the draft materials for the ad campaign arrived, the suggested image would feature a picture of her nearly naked.

Fleshman pushed back, rewriting the copy and saying she would participate if the poster featured her in normal running clothes. This put her endorsement career at risk. But Fleshman said, "I wanted to be a role model to younger girls. I wanted to inspire them to feel powerful and worthy without anyone's approval."

Nike accepted her suggestions, and the poster became iconic. As Fleshman noted, "This wasn't just a shoe poster. It was a statement to young girls of what success looked like."

A doctor and a journalist, Seema Yasmin was frustrated by stories about Muslim women that seem "surprised that we can do things." She notes, "There are still many people who believe Muslim women are One Thing; that we should be This and say That."

Yasmin countered this notion by writing a book entitled *Muslim Women Are Everything: Stereotype-Shattering Stories of Courage, Inspiration, and Adventure.*

The stories she tells in the book show that Muslim women "do everything: fly to space, start multimillion-dollar businesses, get fired from their jobs, jump over hurdles, bake cakes, take naps, wake up late, and do it over again."

The telling is important to Yasmin because she believes "sentences can change the world." She observes, "We write so our stories can be passed on, like chromosomes, to those who will come after, knowing that words spark joy and books ignite revolutions."

71
READ A BOOK,
READ A MIND.

You may not walk in their shoes, but you can borrow them.

Literature allows exploration of alternative identities. As Professor Paula Moya says, "Reading a novel can expand a reader's horizon of possibility for experiential encounters even further than the realm of friendship can." A complex work allows you to enter "another, and ... possibly quite alien, world."

Novels offer a way to understand lived experiences, which can change people's perceptions and attitudes. Moya argues this means "literature written by racial and cultural minorities can play a crucial role in the expansion of people's epistemic [i.e., cognitive] and emotional horizons."

Moya is realistic, noting, "Literature by itself will never change the world or create racial literacy." She's also optimistic, arguing literature "remains a highly powerful tool, and an important actor, in the ongoing struggle to imagine ... another way to be human and free."

Waka Brown's memoir *While I Was Away* shows how this can work.

When she was twelve, Brown went from Kansas to Japan to live for a time with her grandmother (Obaasama). Her memoir tells a story of cultural displacement, adolescence, and growth.

Describing how she felt when leaving her grandmother and Japan, Brown writes:

> *I'm sorry I'm leaving you alone.* I thought of how lonely I often felt these past five months and wept, realizing this was the loneliness Obaasama felt so often during her hard life ... and would feel again now that I was gone.... *I didn't mean for you to love me. I didn't think I would love you, but I do, and I'm so sorry.*

Waka's conclusion holds for those who read her book: "By being away, I traveled to realms in my mind and my heart and soul that I didn't know were even there."

72

SEEING OTHERS SEE YOU IS A BURDEN.

Expectations come from somewhere.

Psychologist Claude Steele studies a particular type he terms "*identity contingencies*—the things you have to deal with in a situation because you have a given social identity, because you are old, young, gay, a white male, a woman, black, Latino, politically conservative or liberal, diagnosed with bipolar disorder, a cancer patient, and so on."

When you're conscious of categories others place you in, it can be distracting and discouraging. Steele says the imposition of "our social identities can strongly affect things as important as our performances in the classroom and on standardized tests, our memory capacity, our athletic performance, the pressure we feel to prove ourselves, even the comfort level we have with people of different groups."

The good news is, understanding how others faced frustrations but eventually found happiness and belonging can help you relax and succeed in college.

The advantage of education itself can be unsettling.

Jesmyn Ward's mother cleaned houses. One day after school, Ward talked with her mother's employer about studying foreign languages. The employer gave helpful if tone-deaf advice—that is, "The best way to learn is to travel. Immerse yourself."

As her mother swept the floor, Ward became conscious of a divide. She says, "[I remember] how my legs tingled as I sat and looked at my mother as she worked, and how I was aware that the wife was talking to me like an intellectual equal, engaging me, asking me about my college plans. How the privilege of my education, my eventual ascent into another class, was born in the inexorable push of my mother's hands. How unfair it all seemed."

Almost daily her mother repeated one phrase like a prayer: "You will go to college." Ward did, and she went on to become a professor and a best-selling author.

73

IT'S EASY TO SEE ANOTHER AS AN OTHER.

For every us there's a them.

Tam O'Shaughnessy and Sally Ride were partners in business and in life. The world saw only half of that.

Building from Ride's experiences as a physicist and astronaut, they created Sally Ride Science to develop educational materials encouraging girls to study science. They chose to keep their home life private. As O'Shaughnessy put it, "When we started Sally Ride Science, we were just worried that it would affect the growth of the company, the sponsorships.... So we elected to be private about it."

O'Shaughnessy observed, "We both didn't like categories, didn't want to define ourselves by our sexuality. We wanted to be beyond labels."

When Ride died, O'Shaughnessy wrote an obituary. She publicly acknowledged their love and life together in the final line, which read, "In addition to Tam O'Shaughnessy, her partner of twenty-seven years, Sally is survived by..."

Ben Barres grew up mislabeled.

At forty-three, he transitioned from Barbara to Ben. In a letter to colleagues and friends, he explained:

> It is not that I wish I were male, rather, I feel that I already am.... This has been a difficult decision because I risk losing everything of importance to me: my reputation, my career, my friends and even my family.... I'm still going to ... [be] pretty much the same person I always have been—it's just that I am going to be a lot happier.

Afterward, Ben Barres's life and career as a neuroscientist flourished. He became the first transgender scientist elected to the National Academy of Sciences. He was a fierce advocate for women in STEM, noting the discrimination he'd faced as a woman.

Barres observed, "It is hard enough to advance the frontiers of science without having to simultaneously confront a mountain of prejudice."

74

PEOPLE WHO LOOK
THE SAME DON'T
THINK THE SAME.

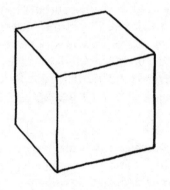

You're unique. So is everyone else.

People often ignore this when they see you as a category rather than a person.

Mae Jemison arrived at college at sixteen. She was a Black woman from a Chicago public school with experience in Russian, physics, and math and an interest in space exploration. But her advisor did not take the time to get to know her. He simply said to take beginner language and regular math. Jemison noted, "He doubted me without bothering to learn anything about me."

When she asked questions in intro chemistry, she said, "[The professor] would either ignore me or act as though I was impossibly dumb for not knowing the answer."

Jemison found mentors, majored in chemical engineering and African and Afro-American studies, and went on to become an astronaut. Her superpower: "Knowing I was worthwhile just because I was me."

As a professor at Yale Law School, Stephen L. Carter has less freedom than many of his colleagues. As Carter puts it, "To be black and an intellectual in America is to live in a box. So I live in a box, not of my own making, and on the box is a label, not of my own choosing."

The "presumptive label reads, 'CAUTION: BLACK LEFT-WING ACTIVIST, HANDLE WITH CARE OR BE ACCUSED OF RACISM.'" But if he criticizes the "dominant civil rights paradigm, the label then becomes, 'CAUTION: BLACK NEOCONSERVATIVE, PROBABLY A NUT CASE.'"

Carter argues if a Black intellectual offers ideas that go against the views expected of a person of color, "then that person is [seen as] not speaking in an authentically black voice."

This can lead to censorship or self-censorship. But Carter notes, "Silencing debate solves no problems; it only limits the range of possible solutions."

75
BE SEEN AND HEARD.

As a CEO in Silicon Valley, Deborah Liu commands attention. But that was not always the case.

Liu says, "I spent most of my life in silence, never speaking up in class or at work." Liu traced part of this to society: "We teach girls not to stand out too much, not to take up too much space." She also told herself, "I'm an introvert."

But when Liu got to business school, half the grade in some courses came from class participation.

Liu chose to treat speaking as a learned skill. She said, "I set a goal of how many times I would participate in each class.... Then I rated myself each time I spoke." She eventually excelled.

Liu observed, "Not giving yourself a free pass means reframing every obstacle as a learning experience." She also learned that "being present means being *heard*."

Allies can help.

Nancy Hamilton was decades older than her classmates when she went back to grad school to study Japanese literature. She notes, "I felt suddenly scrutinized as someone visibly outside the norm."

Self-consciousness translated into self-censorship. She says, "I was surprised by the degree to which my confidence wavered in this new setting."

But she learned, "While there may be no one else like you, there will be people who like you. And that you will like and trust. Let them get to know you."

Camaraderie cultivates confidence.

She says, "When I felt a sense of connection with others in seminar, it gave me the breathing room I needed to break free of self-consciousness and engage more fully."

76

THE RULES OF THE
ROAD ARE UNEVEN.

If you're driving while Black, you fit the description.

The day before she graduated from Harvard with a psychology PhD, Jennifer Eberhardt and a friend were pulled over by a police officer. It turned out the car's registration had expired six weeks earlier. The upshot? The officer slammed her onto the car roof. A tow truck arrived. She ended up chained to a police station wall.

When Eberhardt, who is Black, asked early in the stop what was happening, the officer never answered her questions. She noted, "He didn't want to listen to anything we had to say. He'd decided we were not worthy of his respect."

Charges against her were dismissed. But Eberhardt said of the incident, "[It] did influence my scholarship, by broadening the scope of my work to include the influence of power dynamics and the role of race in the criminal justice process."

As a tenured professor, Brian Lowery enjoys the freedom to dive deep into what interests him. He focuses on how social interactions create notions of identity and self.

As a young Black teenager in Chicago, he had fewer opportunities. One day police approached, hands on their weapons, and asked if they could search him. When Lowery refused, he was handcuffed and charged with resisting arrest.

Looking back, he says, "The police saw me as a potential lawbreaker, which required something of them—that they treat me with suspicion and some degree of fear." Realizing how the police were treating him, Lowery says, "I engaged with them as unjust authorities, which required something of me. It required that I resist their requests."

Interactions like that reduce trust, reveal injustice, and diminish freedom. As Lowery puts it, "In whatever way it changed me, I can never be a person who didn't have that experience."

77

YOUR BACKSTORY
MAY BACK YOU UP.

$$E = h\nu$$

What got you in can get you out.

Darnell Carson grew up homeless. Amid constant moves, he said, "I learned the only thing I could truly rely on, the one thing that couldn't let me down or be ripped away from me, was *me*, my intelligence and my work ethic and whatever shreds of joy I was able to hold onto."

The uncertainty of his youth affected how he approached college. Carson says, "I keep everything organized. . . . I have back-up plans for my back-up plans." Eventually he came to see how plans need to be subject to change. He learned, "The first step to dealing with things that irk or confuse me or leave me in a fog is to accept that they're doing those things."

Though he still operates with a plan, he says, "I've made a lot more room for maybes."

Growing up, Hakeem Oluseyi was on his own. A low point came when, he describes, "Pushing a vacuum cleaner at the Ramada Renaissance wasn't making me enough money. . . . I started scavenging leftover food from the room-service carts people left outside in the hallway."

One summer he landed a research lab job. It was transformative.

As Oluseyi recounts, "Up till that moment, I'd been locked into day-to-day survival questions like How can I eat today? and Where can I find a place to sleep indoors tonight? But now I started to ask myself: What am I really good at, and what could I actually accomplish if I focused my mind on it?"

That research experience led to a PhD program in physics. Oluseyi knew his preparation was weak but said, "I wasn't worried. I may have been the least academically prepared person in my program, but I knew I could outwork anyone."

REFLECTION—
BE YOURSELF.

You arrive and leave college a work in progress.

Like the poet Walt Whitman in *Song of Myself*, you contain multitudes. You have many different social identities. Some are categories you choose, others are imposed on you. You're a new student on campus, an experience shared by the swirl of people moving in. You're also unique, the only one to take your particular road.

Adjusting to college inevitably involves feelings of unease and isolation. Stretching yourself to grow, you'll be meeting new people, trying different extracurriculars, enrolling in topics not taught in high school, and doing this all while missing friends and family.

The temptation is real to go with people who look and think like you as you adjust. If you do that, you're likely to identify the struggles you face as arising primarily from your social identities. Yet as Claude Steele's research on race in college shows, if you engage in conversations with people who are different, you'll discover commonalities. He found when Black and white students shared late-night pizza and updates on their lives, they found similar struggles with grades, teachers, and finances. This was liberating, because it helped them see which difficulties arose from being a college student and which arose from being part of a demographic group.

College is a chance to dive deep into understanding the origins and impacts of race, class, gender, political orientation, and the many other ways that people identify or are categorized. History, literature, and social science offer classes to help you understand how these factors affect people and communities.

Diversity in life experiences and viewpoints leads to better discussions and decisions. The challenge when you're talking across differences is to deeply listen. If you're letting someone speak simply to rebut them, you're closing off your own mind. If you treat someone simply as a representative from a group, you're effectively limiting their contribution to the discussion. As law professor Stephen L. Carter noted, because he is Black people impose a narrow range of expectations about the views he can and should hold.

Colleges are part of the real world. Even as you study discrimination, you may experience it on campus as explicit or implicit bias. Learning the origins and impacts of difference can help you see it. Developing a counternarrative can be a way to navigate. Think about the good things you know to be true about yourself, the successes you've had, and the friends on campus and back home who know the real you.

Education comes with its own forms of prejudice. As you grow in knowledge, you gain ways of understanding the world not readily available without rigorous study. The temptation is to look down on people who don't use the language, frameworks, and assumptions of academia. That arrogance is its own form of ignorance, making it possible you'll fail to appreciate the ideas of people without a four-year degree.

Learning involves holding contradictory thoughts at the same time. When you meet someone new at school, their many social identities carry predictions about life experiences, goals, and interests. Yet they are also unique. Acknowledging a person as part of a group and a particular individual is essential to understanding. You want to be seen as yourself, and so do they.

What this means is that when you're in the seminar room or the dining hall and think you understand how another person's life experience has led them to this place, you should pause. The imperfections of reasoning from categories should lead you to view identity with these caveats: not only, not at all, not so fast.

CITIZENSHIP

78
EMBRACE LIBERTY.

You can make others free.

Supreme Court Justice Stephen Breyer noted that his father couldn't join college social organizations "because he was Jewish." Breyer also observed that when colleagues Sandra Day O'Connor and Ruth Bader Ginsburg graduated, they had a hard time finding legal work because they were female.

In a commencement address, Breyer celebrated that the world had changed and opportunities expanded. But he warned, "It is very important to remember that those changes did not occur magically—that they represented individual, and collective, pioneering efforts."

While stories of legal change focus on legislators and judges, Breyer praised the active commitment to democracy by "millions of ordinary citizens"—which includes you.

He called out cynicism and apathy, saying, "If you do not trust the way our government works, make it work better . . . [by] working together to solve the joint problems that we share as a community."

Supreme Court Justice Anthony Kennedy wrote so eloquently about liberty that people read his words aloud, particularly at weddings.

Kennedy wrote the majority Supreme Court opinion that held that the Constitution guarantees the right to same-sex marriage. He argued, "Changed understandings of marriage are characteristic of a Nation where new dimensions of freedom become apparent to new generations, often through perspectives that begin in pleas or protests and then are considered in the political sphere and the judicial process."

He said those who wrote the Constitution and its amendments "entrusted to future generations a charter protecting the right of all persons to enjoy liberty as we learn its meaning."

When you see the phrase *new* or *future generation*, that means you.

To a gathering of graduates, Kennedy stressed they needed to think hard about freedom's role in their lives, concluding, "You cannot protect what you have not learned; you cannot defend what you do not know."

79
DON'T FREE RIDE.

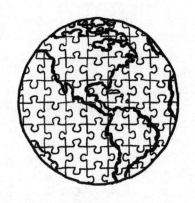

The Party Planning Committee makes *The Office*, and real life, more fun.

College is a collection of events: parties, concerts, games, dinners. Once they're organized, people enjoy them. But somebody needs to take the time to care and organize.

Barry Fischer arrived at school ready to organize, hoping that a college "education would give me the intellectual power to become a real leader, to realize global change." Looking back at graduation, he concluded, "I've come to realize that *I* cannot change the world. But *we* can."

Fischer's experience shifted his view of himself from being "the sum of my actions" to "the sum of my interactions." He grew to see leading as teaming up and connecting.

He ultimately concluded, "Each of us is just a small puzzle piece.... The puzzle that we face is our world, and we need to start working on it right away."

Paul Rogat Loeb's work as a campus political organizer led to a life of social activism. He acknowledges that getting involved in working for change can be frustrating. As he puts it, "Community involvement ... offers no instant miracle cures: 'Save the earth in thirty days. Ask me how.'"

Yet there is a big upside, since "when we do get involved, we get a lot back: new relationships, fresh skills, a sense of empowerment, pride in accomplishment."

Loeb points out that getting involved in community life doesn't require certainty or perfection. You can just "start where you are."

At first, working to change minds, policies, or even leaders can seem daunting. It can involve setbacks and large amounts of time. To persevere, Loeb simply advises,

Savor the journey. Changing the world shouldn't be grim work. Take time to enjoy nature, good music, good conversation, and whatever else lifts your soul.

80
SOMEBODY SHOULD DO SOMETHING.

Could it be you?

When Adam Schiff thought about life after college, he was attracted to the idea of "doctors, nurses, and hospital staff all working toward the unmitigated good of saving lives." His mother was "hoping, like all Jewish mothers, that her son would become a doctor."

He decided instead to go to law school to enter politics.

His parents were disappointed. His mother had "a deep-seated distrust of politics and thought it was a dirty business." His father saw the attractions of corporate law but noted, "[When] you say that you are interested in politics; that just makes me nauseous."

Schiff knew that politics was "contentious, messy, and sometimes corrupt." He also believed it "could bring about systemic change, improving the lives of scores of people." He chose public service, finding impact and fulfillment as an assistant US attorney, state senator, and Congress member.

Powerful and imperfect is how LaDoris Hazzard Cordell viewed the law.

As the first African American woman to serve as a judge in Northern California, Cordell saw failures in justice administration up close. Her assessment: "Bad lawyers, bad jurors, bad judges, uninformed and indifferent voters, opportunistic legislators, and the unconsciously biased all conspire to produce a legal system that way too often does more harm than good for people of color and poor people of any color."

Working in that system as a judge, though, gave her the ability to effect change. She said, "For nearly twenty years, I wielded power over the lives of thousands of people. And ... I did what I believed to be right."

Retired from the bench, she worked on a petition that freed a woman serving an unjust life sentence. Despite its flaws, she said, "I refuse to give up on our legal system."

81

FREE EXPRESSION IS COSTLY AND REWARDING.

If you're here to learn, prepare to be uncomfortable.

That's the message of education school professor Eamonn Callan. He stresses, "There can be no education worth having without the cultivation of the open mind, and an open mind requires a willingness to entertain the possibility that one might be badly wrong on matters of deep conviction or that the offensive speech of another expresses some powerful insight."

When Callan went to college, he did not fit in. He was the first person from his working-class neighborhood to enroll at a university. But gradually he found friends and a great instructor who brought ancient philosophy alive.

Callan valued discussions built on candor, even when offensive. He notes, "The self-respect and confidence I gradually acquired during my years as an undergraduate did not depend on protecting me from the hurt that inevitably comes with open and deep disagreement."

Bad ideas represent a good test for a school's commitment to free expression.

When Stephen L. Carter was in college, a Nobel physicist was trying to give campus talks about his demonstrably inaccurate views on race, intelligence, and policy.

Many academics said his "ideas did not bear discussion . . . because they were perceived to be dangerous."

Carter, who went on to become a law professor, disagreed. He said, "I, too, wanted his ideas to be false, but I wanted them to be *shown* to be false." So he went to a campus debate featuring the controversial physicist, where a geneticist successfully refuted the physicist's flawed arguments.

A takeaway for Carter was that "the mere fact that . . . theories were unattractive should have had no bearing on whether they were accepted as true." Exposing harmful ideas to debate is the best way to reveal errors, change minds, and make progress.

82
ATTACK IDEAS, NOT PEOPLE.

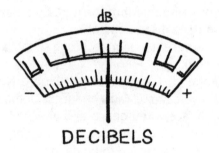

DECIBELS

Your opponents are not your enemies.

But that's not the way it feels in a polarized classroom. Law school student Tess Winston found an "academic environment with two loud camps, one aligning with far-right politics, one aligning with the far left." Most classmates were in the middle—and silent.

Students self-censored because "there's little room for nuance. If you're not overtly one of 'us,' then you're assumed to be one of 'them.'" The implicit message: "Be careful what you say."

In some classes, "students have refused to argue points made by justices whose perspectives they don't like." In another, a student declared, "Being a prosecutor is simply evil."

Winston urged classmates to be the change they want to see, to "speak their piece rather than remaining silent, taking back the room with the sort of thoughtful exchanging of views that is essential to the legal profession."

The pressure to sort the world based on politics starts at home.

Political scientist Shanto Iyengar studies how a person's identification with a political party has become central to social identity. His findings are stark: "Ordinary Americans increasingly dislike and distrust those from the other party. Democrats and Republicans both say that the other party's members are hypocritical, selfish, and close-minded, and they are unwilling to socialize across party lines."

When Iyengar and Matthew Tyler examined survey data from parents and children aged eleven to seventeen, they found, "Polarized parents seem to transmit not only their partisanship, but also their animus toward opponents." In other words, distrust of people you disagree with begins at home.

As you start college, you get to make many choices for yourself. If you resist the idea that people from another party are flawed or wildly misinformed, you will discover new friends and new ideas.

83
RIGHTS COME WITH RESPONSIBILITIES.

You can't have one without the other.

Journalist Ted Koppel has long explored what's interesting and important in politics and society. His takeaway is, "We will not change what's wrong with our culture through legislation, or by choosing up sides on the basis of personal popularity or party affiliation. We will change it by small acts of courage and kindness; by recognizing, each of us, his or her own obligation to set a proper example."

Koppel stresses that you need to recognize how your individual actions affect others as you live in a community. As he told graduating students, "There's no mystery here. You know what to do."

His advice was clear, though challenging: "Aspire to decency. . . . Apply a rigid standard of morality to your lives; and if, periodically, you fail—as you surely will—adjust your lives, not the standards."

What this means is taking to heart the bumper-sticker phrase "Think globally, act locally."

It's easy for Stephen L. Carter to inventory how we ignore civic obligations: "We do not vote in the local elections that affect our daily lives far more than the contests over the Congress and the Presidency that occupy our attention. We do not know the names of our city council members. (We do not even know the names of our neighbors.)"

A better path involves listening to people and being open to persuasion.

You also need to acknowledge, "*Sometimes the other side wins.*" As Carter puts it, integrity involves admitting "we lost not because of some shameless manipulation by our villainous opponents, and not because of some failure to get our message across, but because our fellow citizens, a basically rational bunch, considered both our views and those of the other side and decided that they liked the other side's better."

84
UNIVERSITIES ARE IMPERFECT.

Schools are like people. You can love them and still hope they change.

Universities make difficult decisions about worker pay, campus energy sources, and endowment investments. When senior Courtney Cooperman examined her school's choices, she found it was "complicit in many of the problems that it claims to equip its students to solve."

Yet she loved her college life. She said, "[The school's] complicity in injustice does not detract from the joy and purposefulness that I felt nearly every single day of my undergraduate career.... I still felt a sense of magic every time I biked through Main Quad at sunset . . . or walked home from a lecture that made me look at the world in a new light."

She resolved as an alum to be proud when the school "acts as a force for good in the world, and vocal when it falls short."

Today's student protestors may be tomorrow's politicians.

When students occupied the university president's office to protest draft policies during the Vietnam War, freshman Mitt Romney joined a counterprotest, carrying a sign saying "Speak Out Don't Sit In."

Romney's future presidential opponent Barack Obama made his first public political speech at a campus rally, urging his school to stop investing in companies that operated in South Africa's apartheid economy.

As seniors, Susan Rice and Michael McFaul helped create an alumni fund, with the money only going to the school if it divested from firms doing business in South Africa or if apartheid ended.

When Rice went to a graduation weekend event, the university president "paused to berate me and condemn our initiative as destructive to the university." Rice said her parents had a different reaction, since they were "proud that I was kicking up some righteous dust on my way out the door."

85

YOU BEND THE ARC.

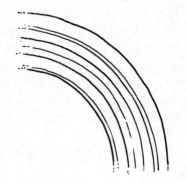

In his final Sunday-morning sermon, Martin Luther King Jr. said, "The arc of the moral universe is long, but it bends toward justice."

Gravity doesn't pull the world toward fairness. You do.

As law professor Pamela Karlan told a gathering of first-year college students, "Part of your job is to be the kind of people who pull on that arc and bend it toward more justice, more liberty, more equality, and more dignity for people."

Working at the Department of Justice, Karlan cited the inspiration of Fannie Lou Hamer, who was jailed and beaten while promoting Black voter registration.

Karlan noted, "It is because of valiant women of the vote like her, who refused to be silenced even when they were sick and tired, that the United States has come closer to the Constitution's aspiration of 'securing the Blessing of Liberty' to *all* 'our posterity.'"

Sitting on the sidelines was not an option George Shultz chose.

Shultz famously had a tie, given to him by Ronald Reagan, which read, "Democracy is not a spectator sport." Shultz drew upon his expertise in economics and business to serve in government as secretary of labor, director of the Office of Management and Budget, secretary of the treasury, and secretary of state.

Those are high-profile jobs, but Shultz warned about their temptations. He said, "You cannot want the job too much. If you do, you tend to cut and fit, and can all too easily lose your way. You must be willing to stake out a position and stand there when overriding issues of principle are at stake."

Power brings opportunities to change the world, but whether that's for good or ill depends on you. As Shultz notes, "Public service works only if . . . you are true to yourself."

REFLECTION—
LISTEN AND ACT.

When leaders talk about the future, that's you.

For nearly two decades you've been guided by institutions, algorithms, and policies designed and operated by adults. This division of labor means you've had the freedom to grow as a person without contributing much to political life. That calculus changes as you register to vote, move away from family, and join a campus community.

College is filled with memorable events—parties, plays, trips, special dinners. Once those are organized, they're a chance to draw closer to classmates and savor life. Someone, though, has to step up and take the time to plan these gatherings.

That's a challenge confronting communities of any size. The temptation is to sit back and let others organize an event or agree on a policy. Once that's done, you can often enjoy the benefits whether or not you helped contribute to its creation. The logic of collective action means you may sit back and free ride, counting on others to create experiences you'll enjoy.

People who value living in their community reject that logic. You might act out of a sense of responsibility, believing that you have a duty to contribute. You could enjoy the psychic rewards of leadership, the sense of accomplishment in moving people toward a larger goal. You may simply enjoy working with others, making friends as you help solve a problem.

Colleges, like states, are laboratories of democracy. Extracurriculars generate political skills through the learning-by-doing involved in fundraising, publicizing, and organizing. Courses in history, political science, economics, and philosophy offer intellectual frameworks that help you develop a political world view. Conversations with friends can model how to listen with an open mind and a willingness to change.

Over time I've seen the college experiences of classmates translate into political action and public service. A friend from my first-year dorm now appears regularly on the House floor, quoting writings of the Founders he read in government courses. Fellow econ majors have used their abilities to frame trade-offs to serve on the Federal Reserve, help run a school board, and offer policy advice to the governor of California. A college roommate known for his willingness to call out inequality in the law now serves as a tribal court judge.

I've seen former students develop interests in college that led to public impact. A civil engineering and public policy major who wrote his thesis on Mississippi River flood control went on to become CEO of a clean energy company. A student asking questions in office hours about developing a better system for newspaper advertising founded a software company whose products power government agencies, NGOs, and companies. A student fascinated by the coalition assembled by Robert F. Kennedy went on to run a presidential campaign in a swing state. My former students have run for governor, state legislator, and school board member positions and staffed government offices and campaigns.

Participating in politics takes many forms—voting, organizing, donating, even running for office. Other forms of community service offer similar ways to contribute through volunteering. What these opportunities share is a chance to make a difference in the lives of friends and family and in the lives of people you may never meet.

Pathways into government carry less certainty than traditional careers. They can depend on elections and on changing public agendas. You may choose to limit your participation to voting. If you do end up in public service at some point in your life, the chance to help others is hard to match.

The public interest does not write checks. But its pursuit can be highly rewarding.

HOW TO
GO WRONG

86

DON'T . . . SIMPLY
FOLLOW THE MARKET.

Your distraction builds fortunes, though your life is poorer for it.

Content on your phone is supported by advertising. Selling your attention makes social media possible. Online images and attitudes are engaging, even addictive. And as you scroll, you're seeing ads meant to change what you believe, want, and buy.

Your value as a consumer affects your life as a student. Lectures are challenging; discovering ideas through reading is difficult. It's much easier to switch from education to entertainment. You can see this in class as people surf the web and text.

Nir Eyal, who writes about markets and psychology, puts it starkly: "In the future, there will be two kinds of people in the world: those who let their attention be controlled and coerced by others and those who proudly call themselves 'indistractable.'" Turning off your phone in class is one way to reclaim your focus.

Gil Fronsdal thinks about distraction for a living, since he teaches meditation.

Curating experiences and posting about your life online is exhausting. As Fronsdal notes, "Maintaining and defending a self-image can be a lot of work. It can fuel a lot of self-conscious pre-occupation with how we speak, dress, and behave."

The media's celebration of fame and influence crowds out many joys. As Fronsdal puts it, "The values of contentment, peace, generosity, love and compassion . . . can be in conflict with the values of consumerism, ambition, selfishness and insensitivity found in much of our popular culture."

Recognizing the forces that aim to distract you is a first step. For Fronsdal, next steps involve meditation and mindfulness. He says, "By focusing on simply being aware, we learn to disentangle ourselves from our habitual reactions and begin to have a friendlier and more compassionate relationship with our experience, with ourselves, and with others."

87

DON'T . . . MAXIMIZE LIFETIME INCOME.

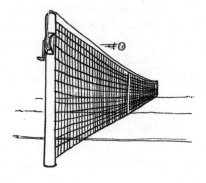

Life is not a job. Your job is not your life.

But it can be easy to think otherwise. Writing *The Good Enough Job*, Simone Stolzoff saw many people who defined their self-worth by their productivity. Yet he made an interesting discovery: "After interviewing hundreds of people and spending many hours with the central characters of this book, I found those with the healthiest relationships to their work had one thing in common: they all had a strong sense of who they were when they weren't working."

Finding that takes effort. Stolzoff notes, "To detach our sense of self-worth from our work . . . we must first develop a self that no boss or job title or market has the power to change."

Stolzoff suggests starting with the question "What do you *like to* do?" since "that allows you to define yourself on your own terms."

John McEnroe is famous for his work as a Wimbledon champion, tennis commentator, and narrator for *Never Have I Ever*.

His advice to graduating seniors may seem surprising: "Everyone wants a great career, but don't miss your life on the way to work. Work/life balance may seem impossible, but it's worth pursuing."

At a time in life when people may overwork, he reminded graduates, "You are the sum of your WHOLE life, not your professional accomplishments. So start enjoying life now. Don't wait till your career takes off."

As you progress through college, friends and family start asking about future employment. This generates a focus on salaries, titles, and career plans. McEnroe offers another way to keep score: "Don't get crushed under the weight of your expectations. Know that the real victory in life is the long game—measure your success by how much you evolve, not necessarily how much you win."

88
DON'T . . . PURSUE RESUME VIRTUES.

Some days you value the most won't make your resume.

As an English professor, Terry Castle can both understand and satirize her students' rush to build "supersize CV's." She writes that their resumes need to "advertise a catalog of competencies: your diverse interests, original turn of mind, ability to work alone or in a team, time-management skills, enthusiasm, unflappability—not to mention your moral probity, generosity to those less fortunate, lovable 'meet cute' quirkiness, and pleasure in the simple things of life, such as synchronized swimming, competitive dental flossing, and Antarctic exploration."

Her students also say "they can barely keep up ... particularly given all the texting and tweeting and cellphoning they have to do from hour to hour."

Castle contrasts the piling up of extracurriculars with what she experienced in college: "Reading books, listening to music, falling in love (or at least imagining it)."

As a business school dean, Jon Levin led a faculty focused on helping graduates navigate markets.

But he also believes students should learn how to live a good life. That includes thinking about happiness, "the idea that we are fulfilled through friendships and experiences that bring joy and pleasure." Levin notes it includes a search for meaning, the idea that "we should seek to have a purpose and commit ourselves to that purpose."

Levin points out that "when people reflect back late in life, what they regret is usually not the things they've done or failed at, but the things they haven't done." Research reveals, "Living a good life means that we keep seeking new experiences, and keep finding new perspectives or ways to think about the world."

Levin, now a university president, believes a successful education can teach you "to broaden your perspective, to take risks, to seek new experiences, to live a psychologically rich life."

89

DON'T . . . EXPECT TO KNOW YOUR LIFE PLAN RIGHT NOW.

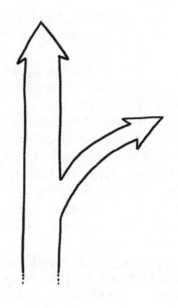

As you change, your mind does too.

As Jesmyn Ward worked a series of unsatisfying jobs after graduation, she came to a realization: "Completing university was not an ending, but instead was the beginning of finding my way to doing something meaningful. I learned that for most of us, there are no easy, singular ascents, and I realized I wanted to be a writer."

For several years she read. She got a master of fine arts degree. She taught. She wrote stories, faced rejection, and revised. Eventually, she found a publisher and a wide audience.

Ward notes that for some, "Success comes after thousands of hours of work, and lucky breaks, and study, and heartbreak, and loss, and wandering. As an adult, I learned this: persist, work hard, face rejection, and weather the setbacks until you meet a gatekeeper who will open a door for you."

John Hennessy's progress through academia looks logical and linear: professor, dean, provost, and president. But that's not a path he foresaw.

Hennessy says, "You don't have to know, when you are young, who you want to be.... You're creating that destination— and yourself—as you go."

He has clear advice for graduates: "The early years of your career should be devoted to doing the best job you can in your chosen profession—building your skills, gaining experience, establishing yourself as an individual and team member. No one knows what opportunities may follow from there."

The value he places on meaning and purpose is clear from a quotation he cites from Reverend Peter Gomes: "Your whole object here is not to make a living but it is to make a life that is worth living." Hennessy believes that advice goes unheeded because most students are "just too young to get it."

90

DON'T . . . HAVE THE EXPERIENCE, MISS THE MEANING.

To understand the world, you need to be there.

As a senior in high school, Michael Tubbs entered an essay contest hosted by the Pulitzer Prize–winning novelist Alice Walker. He wrote about his mother's perseverance and his father's imprisonment. He described life in the impoverished city of Stockton, California.

Ten years later, he became mayor of that city. His political rise involved thinking hard about community. He saw this reflection as a power: "Storytelling—truth-telling—is how we make sense of the world as it is and gain the vision and courage to create the world as it should be."

Tubbs won the writing contest, with Alice Walker noting, "Tubbs' essay exemplifies what *The Color Purple* is about: the belief that each of us has an indomitable spirit within us that we can trust to carry us through perils."

If you miss the experience, it is hard to find its meaning.

Music professor Mark Applebaum's students are highly talented. But some fail to come to class, missing out on the chance to contribute to discussion and engage directly with ideas.

This frustrates Applebaum, who believes "showing up—and on time—is kind of a big deal." As he puts it, "There are very few music prodigies who get a chance if they are late (whether late to a gig or by a 16th note)."

His advice to students applies broadly to college life: "Turn in assignments on time; respond to email in a timely manner; attend a lecture without the distraction of an electronic device; be on time to class; follow assignment instructions."

Applebaum is not a traditionalist. He teaches a class entitled *Rock, Sex, and Rebellion*, which celebrates iconoclasm. He knows, though, that focus, thoughtfulness, and attendance are essential skills in life.

91

DON'T...
AVOID CHALLENGING
PLEASURES.

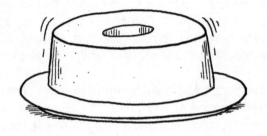

It's easier to read an ad than a poem, and that's by design.

Armed with an MBA, Dana Gioia gained success marketing Jell-O. He understood how commercial entertainment revolves around selling. Gioia observed, "Entertainment promises us a predictable pleasure—humor, thrills, emotional titillation, or even the odd delight of being vicariously terrified. It exploits and manipulates who we are rather than challenges us with a vision of who we might become."

Gioia wrote poetry at night. Eventually, he quit business to become a writer of poems, essays, and operas. Speaking to graduates about his experiences in advertising and art, he posed this question: "Do you want to watch the world on a screen or live in it so meaningfully that you change it?"

Making the case for art, he said, "There are some truths about life that can be expressed only as stories, or songs, or images."

An alum three years out of college sees a similar connection between challenging yourself and moving forward in life. Reflecting on college, she says:

> It was a place so beautiful yet so daunting. So fun yet so challenging. So happy yet so depressing. So forward-thinking yet so stagnant. So inclusive yet so divisive. So big yet so insular. And all the words in between. These words taught me nuance—which changed how I experienced life going forth.

Noting that "forging genuine connections takes lots of work," she credits college for bringing and continuing to bring "many interesting people into my life. And that makes life more fun."

Life after graduation involves new experiences with moves, jobs, and relationships. She notes that college "was one of the more challenging things I've done in life. And the thing with doing hard things—you know you will likely be able to do other hard things too."

92

DON'T . . .
STAY BUSY.

Daily Planner

Monday

SCHEDULE

9:00 AM	Sales Meeting
10:00 AM	Zoom w/ Clients
11:00 AM	Focus Group
12 NOON	TRAIL RUN!
1:00 PM	Production Meeting
2:00 PM	Product Launch
3:00 PM	Design Session w/Client
4:00 PM	Marketing Seminar
5:00 PM	Employee Review

Why the rush?

Author Jenny Odell notes that the drive for efficiency raises a simple question: What are you saving time for? She hopes that people are "spending less time on things that you don't want to be doing so that you can do things you've decided are meaningful to you."

When asked how she defines the meaning of life, Odell says, "I want to be in contact with things, people, contexts that make me feel alive. I have a specific definition of alive, which is I want to feel like I am being changed."

Conversation can change your mind. Walking in nature can show you evolving life. Experiences like these remind Odell, "I'm alive, today is not the same as yesterday, I will be different in the future, therefore I have a reason to live, which is to find out what that change is going to be."

Speaking at commencement, actor Sterling K. Brown offered a warning from Socrates: "Beware the barrenness of a busy life."

He told graduates, "There will be an enormous pull when you enter into the real world to be busy. Always doing, always hustling and bustling." As a counter, he asked, "Have you contemplated the importance of stillness? Is being busy the same as being productive?"

Brown praised goals and striving for personal excellence. He warned against perfectionism and obsession with a destination. He recommended instead enjoying the journey, "knowing that there will always be endless room for improvement."

Brown concluded, "If you still fool yourself into thinking the end point of perfection is something that exists, and can be attained, I worry that you may miss the beautiful curve of a life well lived, never enjoying where you are in the moment, always wishing you were someplace, something, or someone else."

93

DON'T . . . GRIND.

Car gears don't work well if you grind too much. The same is true of people.

Ancient Chinese philosophy and modern science make the same point—it's possible to try too hard. In *Trying Not to Try*, Edward Slingerland draws upon both to demonstrate the benefits of sometimes stepping back. He points out, "When one is stymied by a problem, simply leaving it alone and doing something else is often the best way to solve it."

Slingerland makes this case: "Doing nothing allows your unconscious to take over, and ... the unconscious is often better at solving certain types of particularly complex problems."

Shifting attention away from monitoring and measuring yourself also helps you engage with others. Slingerland notes, "Actually *caring* about the conversation instead of reflecting on whether you can contribute to it or consciously monitoring how people are reacting to you is what's really important."

As a research psychologist and exercise instructor, Kelly McGonigal has thought about how people can set aside the grind. She notes, "Over the years, I saw again and again how movement could shift a person's mood. How it could send someone back into the world renewed with hope."

McGonigal stresses how group exercise is "a way to practice self-care, an opportunity to tackle challenges, and a place to make friends."

There's an added bonus if your movement is outside. McGonigal reports, "Natural environments have the ability to instill feelings of what researchers call *prospect*—an elevated perspective and hopefulness, often triggered by natural beauty or awe-inspiring views—and *refuge*, the sense of being sheltered or protected."

She makes the case that movement produces "short-lived feelings of pleasure or pride" and a "happiness that comes from having a sense of purpose and belonging. The happiness of feeling connected to something bigger than yourself."

94

DON'T . . .
PURSUE PERFECTION.

The road to perfection is a dead end.

Tennis champion John McEnroe knows that some believe "winning is everything." He says that "in reality, it's not." Instead, "The questions you have to answer are: 'Am I getting better as a person?' And, 'Is what I'm doing bringing me and the ones around me happiness?'"

Trying something new can be daunting. But McEnroe says, "It's very important for people who are high-flying ... to realize that taking risks, failing, and learning from your failures is essential to your development. And sometimes a loss is the best thing that can happen to you."

What matters is being in the arena. McEnroe says in tennis, you have a split second to make decisions: "Sometimes you win the point and sometimes it's an endless rally that you lose. But you take your best shot and keep finding the courage to step on the court."

In high school, Gretchen Carlson was aiming for a 4.0.

One day an English teacher returned her paper with two words, *Carpe diem*, in place of a grade. She realized he'd written "seize the day" to "make me think out of the box instead of just always expecting a perfect grade. He was challenging me to open myself to opportunities."

In college, Carlson earned her first C. The experience taught her "that life wasn't a series of perfect moves, that working hard was important, but that sometimes it didn't create the desired result."

Carlson went on to win the Miss America title, work as a journalist at CBS News and Fox News, and write several books. Some told her, "It's easy for you. You're perfect."

Carlson knew otherwise. She knew her limitations but said, "I embrace my imperfections, knowing I don't have to be perfect to follow my dreams."

95

DON'T...
LET FEAR, OF FAILURE
OR MISSING OUT, DRIVE.

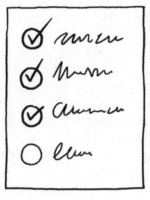

Expect the unexpected.

Following plans got you to college. But there can be too much of a good thing. Psychologist Elissa Epel notes, "It's very easy to tip over the line from productive planning into wheel spinning that wears us out, tanks our mood."

Epel champions uncertainty. She says, "When you embrace, 'I don't know,' you stop clinging to an outcome, you drop the narrative of catastrophic outcomes, and you open yourself up to the range of possible outcomes."

She realistically assesses risk. Rather than obsessing about the worst outcome, she advises, "Focus on what's *probable*, not what's *possible*."

Her pro tip: "I have developed a lifelong habit of making a to-do list and putting it aside, as part of my nightly wind-down ritual. That way I don't spend sleep time reciting my list or adding to it, trying to control the future."

Looking back as a senior, Grace Carroll sees planning differently.

She notes, "When I arrived at college, I arrived with a very sure story about the world and how I fit into it. I'm beginning to think that the real value of a college education is the slow undoing of your most firmly-held truths."

Carroll as a frosh had goals relating to prestige and prizes. Yet as she watched classmates pursue jobs with high pay and uncertain rewards, she started to see her "friends make choices out of fear but call it ambition."

Reflecting on college, Carroll lists highlights not found on a resume: sunsets with friends, days hiking or spearfishing, a gallery afternoon. Those moments of joy led her to this advice for her frosh self: "You have the rest of your life to win prizes. . . . But you have one specific chance to be nineteen, twenty, twenty-one, twenty-two."

96

DON'T . . .
GO WITH YOUR
FIRST IDEA.

The hardest bias to spot is your own.

Questioning what you know is central to your education. As Louis Newman writes in *Thinking Critically in College*, "Part of the challenge of college is gradually, with repeated practice, becoming more adept at asking increasingly interesting and useful questions."

Newman notes, "Developing a habit of considering alternatives to everything you encounter in college . . . will also make you aware of your own biases, which sometimes lead you to be less critical of positions with which you already agree."

This can be difficult: "No one wants to discover that something they have long believed is actually mistaken." Newman points out that the "readiness, even eagerness, to challenge your established views requires a kind of intellectual courage."

Learning is questioning, since "all knowledge is discovered and refined through exploring context, considering alternatives, weighing evidence, and finding implications and new applications."

As a designer, Ashish Goel knows the value of building a prototype.

This often involves starting with a version that's rough, flawed, and clunky. But Goel knows imperfection is the basis of progress. As he puts it:

> The first pancake always ends up in the trash. The lesson applies whether you're talking about breakfast or passion projects. Being willing to create bad work first in order to create good work later on is not just an act of courage (taking a risk for something that matters); it really is the only way to create at all, and the only way to get used to fear in all of its shapeshifting avatars.

He notes that trying something new can take many forms: raising your hand in class, saying hello to a stranger, or starting work that's initially bad. Sharing your draft ideas and projects with others becomes the path to improvement.

97
DON'T...
SEEK WHAT'S
COMFORTABLE.

You don't know what you don't know.

As a psychologist who studies happiness, Emma Seppala knows that many popular ideas about what generates success in life are false. One misguided piece of advice she identifies is "Focus on your niche," which translates into a strategy of "Immerse yourself in your area of knowledge."

Another adage she refutes is "Play to your strengths." This notion leads to a simple rule of thumb: "Align your work with your talents. Do what you do best, and stay away from your weak areas."

These strategies are the wrong way to approach college. Instead, you should take classes in areas you've never explored. Join clubs focused on activities involving new experiences. Meet people whose lives generate different ways for you to understand the world. If you see college as a chance to sample and stretch, you'll move beyond your high school self.

College offers the chance to try on new social roles: community member, voter, activist, leader.

Working to change minds or policies can be challenging. Paul Loeb writes about how some individuals go from campus politics into a life of community involvement. For these people, Loeb notes, "Social activism gives them a sense of purpose, pride, and service; teaches them new skills; shows them how to confront daunting obstacles; and lets them experience new worlds."

Loeb also finds the work of those involved in community efforts "offers camaraderie and helps them build powerful friendships, partnerships, and sometimes romances."

You can join with other people to create events and bring about change at many levels of community: your dorm, college, state, or even country. The larger the radius you're working in, the more difficult the odds. But Loeb notes, "There's no greater antidote to powerlessness than joining with others in common cause."

98
DON'T . . .
GET SERIOUS.

It is a laughing matter.

Alejandro Salinas's college career began off campus on a week-long hiking trip. Looking back as a senior, he wrote, "That backpacking trip was my first taste of what the next four years would turn out to be like: a collection of memories forged together by laughter, humility, and teamwork."

On the trip's last night, the hikers penned letters to their senior selves. Salinas wrote, "I have had a wonderful time laughing with these guys. I can't imagine what the next 4 years will hold."

Salinas eagerly sought out new friends and experiences. He was dorm co-president, wrote for the paper, and rushed a fraternity. He says, "In each of those communities, I met incredible, genuine individuals, motivated and driven to share their passions and build meaningful relationships."

And as a senior he noted, "The last four years have gone by faster than I could have imagined."

Jennifer Aaker and Naomi Bagdonas teach a business school course on the value of humor.

Using evidence from academic articles and case studies, they make the case that humor "fosters meaningful connections, unlocks creativity, makes tense situations less stressful, and helps us survive and thrive through life's ups and downs."

In their book *Humor, Seriously*, Aaker and Bagdonas emphasize how in humor and in a well-lived life, "boldness, authenticity, presence, joy, and love flourish." They frequently quote comedians in the book about the nature and impact of comedy. They end with a quotation from Stephen Colbert:

> In my experience, you will truly serve only what you love.
> If you love friends, you will serve friends. If you love community, you will serve your community. If you love money, you will serve money. And if you love only yourself, you will serve only yourself, and you will have only yourself.

99
DON'T...
IGNORE YOUR
ANCESTORS.

If you know how you got here, you can see where to go.

Julian Castro's career path started generations ago. He said, "My grandmother spent her whole life working as a maid, a cook, and a babysitter, barely scraping by, but still working hard to give my mother, her only child, a chance in life, so that my mother could give my brother and me an even better one."

Castro's mother took him and his twin Joaquin to campaign rallies as children, telling them, "If something is wrong, you change it. Your efforts may pay off in the long run, even if you don't get your way right now." Both ended up graduating from law school. Julian became mayor of San Antonio, his brother a Congress member.

Looking at his family's path, Castro concluded that "the American dream is not a sprint, or even a marathon, but a relay."

Cory Booker's journey in politics also started generations ago.

When Booker graduated from college, his grandfather told him, "This degree you hold, you earned it through your hard work; be proud of that. But you can't forget—don't you ever forget—that it was also paid for by the blood, sweat, and tears of your ancestors."

Pointing to civil rights activists, Booker's mother reminded him, "This person marched for you. This person protested for you. This person sacrificed and risked expulsion for you."

Booker took these messages to heart, saying, "Actions, small and large, radiate out into eternity. What we do or fail to do ... leaves a lasting imprint." In his work as mayor of Newark and later a senator from New Jersey, Booker focused on policies with impacts reaching far into the future. He notes, "We do owe a debt that we can't pay back but must pay forward."

100
DON'T . . .
PUT IT OFF.

Start now.

College involves uncertainty. You're in a new place, surrounded by different people, tackling challenging topics.

Bernie Roth knows risk and uncertainty can freeze students, preventing them from trying new experiences. So he makes grappling with a personal challenge a project in his design class. The assignment: "Do something you have really wanted to do and have never done, or solve a problem in your life."

For Roth, a basic design principle is bias toward action, the idea that "it is better to start to do something and fail than it is to do nothing and wait for the correct path of action to appear."

You might succeed. If not, "you do, you fail, you learn. You do again, you fail again, and you learn some more." Across many areas of life, Roth observes, "If you are mindful about what you have done, failure is a teacher."

As an improv teacher, Patricia Madson's favorite word is YES, a word that allows "you to enter a new world, a world of action, possibility, and adventure."

Getting to yes can be hard. For students uncertain about where to begin, she counsels, "Start anywhere. . . . All starting points are equally valid." To students facing an unknown outcome, she advises, "Substitute attention for what *is* happening for attention to what *might* happen."

Madson says, "We often substitute planning, ruminating, or list-making for actually doing something about our dreams. . . . The habit of excessive planning impedes our ability to see what is actually in front of us."

You've made it through high school, navigated applying, and gotten in. Now is the time to start living your best life in college. Or as Madson puts it, "Change the habit of getting ready for life in favor of getting on with it now."

REFLECTION—
GET READY TO CHANGE.

Education should equip you to entertain three things: an idea, yourself, and a friend.

I read that adage on a college application during my senior year in high school, and it stuck. It means your time in college promises to enhance your future life. You'll learn how to learn. You'll discover ideas and experiences that make your life more interesting. You'll also gain the ability to share insights so friends appreciate even more the chance to be with you.

There are many people vying for your attention on campus. Advertisers wrap their messages around engaging content, hoping to transform you into a customer. Employers promote internships and first jobs as valuable on-ramps to careers.

Market messages often emphasize the instrumental value of education. Learning is pursued because of where it can take you, not as something good in and of itself. The good news is that if you follow what you value intrinsically, it can often help you instrumentally.

What does this mean? Consider three examples. If you study what you find inherently interesting in college, you'll often excel. That can translate into better critical thinking skills and higher achievements, outcomes sought by future employers. If you take the time to get to know people, you'll develop enduring friendships. You'll also have a future network to draw on for career advice. If you treat sleep and exercise as priorities, you'll be both happier and more productive.

After graduation you'll spend at least a third of your time during the week at work. Your education prepares you to find financial success, meaning, and impact during those thousands of hours. Firms devote significant effort to recognizing and rewarding the skills that make those hours productive.

Your nights and weekends, though, don't have a human resources department. You're on your own to learn how college can prepare you to get the most out of the majority of your life, the time when you're not at work.

Your future self could tell you how time away from a grinding focus on school pays off. Going out with friends or staying in to talk yields memories. In the long run, you get to revisit these years in your mind and reconnect with those friends. Just as you shared the challenges and thrills of adjusting to college, you'll similarly go through other life events with these friends—marriage, children, job changes, and more.

Move-in day is filled with uncertainty and ambiguity. You'll miss friends from high school but know that somewhere on campus are your future classmates and companions. You'll feel the same mix of feelings on graduation day as friends disperse and you head off too.

What will be different is you. Through the courses you take and the friends you make, you'll become better at living with uncertainty and seeking out new experiences. You'll have learned a key takeaway from college too—life is more essay than short answer. For the most important questions, there aren't simple, one-word solutions.

Many lessons in this book come from personal narratives about the impact of college. These bear out the insight that life is lived forward but understood backward. The beauty of both memoirs and social science research is that you can learn from the experiences of others. Insights from this book, like the courses you will take in college, are designed to help you see, experience, and change the world.

If you embrace life on campus as a chance to explore new ideas, people, and adventures, you'll get the best that college has to offer—an education and a degree.

NOTES BY LESSON

1. Anthony P. Carnevale, Ban Cheah, and Emma Wenzinger, *The College Payoff: More Education Doesn't Always Mean More Earnings* (Washington, DC: Georgetown University Center on Education and the Workforce, 2021), 3; Michael Spence, "Job Market Signaling," *Quarterly Journal of Economics* 87, no. 3 (1973): 355–74.

2. Carly Fiorina, *Tough Choices: A Memoir* (New York: Portfolio, 2007), 14, 16; Carly Fiorina, "Commencement Address," Stanford University, June 17, 2001, https://news.stanford.edu/2001/06/17/process-distillation-getting-essence -things/; Evan Thomas, *First: Sandra Day O'Connor* (New York: Random House, 2019), 35; Sandra Day O'Connor, *Out of Order: Stories from the History of the Supreme Court* (New York: Random House, 2014), 152.

3. Sterling K. Brown, "Commencement Address," Stanford University, June 17, 2018, https://news.stanford.edu/2018/06/17/2018-commencement -speech-stanford-alumnus-sterling-k-brown/; Cory Booker, *United: Thoughts on Finding Common Ground and Advancing the Common Good* (New York: Ballantine Books, 2017), 124, 126.

4. Steve Jobs, "Commencement Address," Stanford University, June 12, 2005, https://news.stanford.edu/2005/06/12/youve-got-find-love-jobs-says/; Phil Knight, *Shoe Dog: A Memoir by the Creator of Nike* (New York: Simon & Schuster, 2016), 3, 5.

5. Jennifer Summit and Blakey Vermeule, *Action versus Contemplation: Why an Ancient Debate Still Matters* (Chicago: University of Chicago Press, 2018), 22; Paul Kalanithi, *When Breath Becomes Air* (New York: Random House, 2016), 19, 31, 33–34, 149.

6. Randy Komisar and Kent L. Lineback, *The Monk and the Riddle: The Art of Creating a Life While Making a Living* (Boston: Harvard Business Press, 2001), 65, 173; Bill Burnett and Dave Evans, *Designing Your Life: How to Build a Well-Lived, Joyful Life* (New York: Knopf, 2016), xxvii, 33, 94.

7. Bernard Roth, *The Achievement Habit: Stop Wishing, Start Doing, and Take Command of Your Life* (New York: HarperCollins, 2015), 15, 18, 20, 21; Philip Zimbardo and John Boyd, *The Time Paradox: The New Psychology of Time That Will Change Your Life* (New York: Free Press, 2008), 316.

8. bell hooks, *Wounds of Passion: A Writing Life* (New York: Henry Holt and Company, 1997), 152; bell hooks, *All about Love: New Visions* (New York: William Morrow, 2018), 83; Tanya M. Luhrmann, *How God Becomes Real: Kindling the Presence of Invisible Others* (Princeton: Princeton University Press, 2020), x, 79.

9. Ben Barres, *The Autobiography of a Transgender Scientist* (Cambridge, MA: MIT Press, 2020), 4, 5, 59; Kalanithi, *When Breath Becomes Air*, 168, 170–72.

10. William Damon, *The Path to Purpose: How Young People Find Their Calling in Life* (New York: Free Press, 2009), xii, 22, 145; Katie Ledecky, *Just Add Water: My Swimming Life* (New York: Simon & Schuster, 2024), 233.

11. Jobs, "Commencement Address"; John Markoff, *Whole Earth: The Many Lives of Stewart Brand* (New York: Penguin Press, 2022), 373, 375, 377.

12. Gil Fronsdal, *The Issue at Hand: Essays on Buddhist Mindfulness Practice* (Redwood City, CA: Insight Meditation Center, 2008), viii, 45; Personal communication, August 17, 2023.

13. Hart Research Associates, *It Takes More Than a Major: Employer Priorities for College Learning and Student Success* (Washington, DC: Hart Research Associates, 2013), 4; Jaison R. Abel and Richard Deitz, "Agglomeration and Job Matching among College Graduates," *Regional Science and Urban Economics* 51 (2015): 16; US Bureau of Labor Statistics, "Number of Jobs, Labor Market Experience, Marital Status, and Health for Those Born 1957–1964," August 22, 2023, https://www.bls.gov/news.release/pdf/nlsoy.pdf; Stanford BEAM, "Career Truths," accessed August 21, 2024, https://web.archive.org/web/20220521151323/https://beam.stanford.edu/careertruths; Issa Rae, "Commencement Address," Stanford University, June 13, 2021, https://news.stanford.edu/2021/06/13/2021-commencement-address-issa-rae/.

14. Robert M. Sapolsky, *A Primate's Memoir: A Neuroscientist's Unconventional Life among the Baboons* (New York: Touchstone, 2002), 15–16; Guy Kawasaki, *Wise Guy: Lessons from a Life* (New York: Portfolio, 2019), 45.

15. Damon, *Path to Purpose*, 8, 145; Atul Gawande, "Commencement Address," Stanford University, June 12, 2021, https://news.stanford.edu/2021/06/12/2021-commencement-address-dr-atul-gawande/.

16. Emma Seppala, *The Happiness Track: How to Apply the Science of Happiness to Accelerate Your Success* (New York: HarperCollins, 2017), 27; Sami Jo Small, *The Role I Played: Canada's Greatest Olympic Hockey Team* (Toronto: ECW Press, 2020), 9, 79.

17. Blakey Vermeule, "In Their Own Words: Why Do We Care about Literary Characters?," *Stanford Report*, December 7, 2022, https://news.stanford.edu/report/2022/12/07/why-do-we-care-about-literary-characters/; Shankar Vedantam and Bill Mesler, *Useful Delusions: The Power and Paradox of the Self-Deceiving Brain* (New York: W. W. Norton & Company, 2021), 201.

18. John L. Hennessy, *Leading Matters: Lessons from My Journey* (Stanford: Stanford University Press, 2018), 5, 121, 122; Sam Wineburg, *Why Learn History (When It's Already on Your Phone)* (Chicago: University of Chicago Press, 2018), 78.

19. David Deming, "In the Salary Race, Engineers Sprint but English Majors Endure," *New York Times*, September 20, 2019, https://www.nytimes.com/2019/09/20/business/liberal-arts-stem-salaries.html; Debra Humphreys and Patrick Kelly, *How Liberal Arts and Sciences Majors Fare in Employment: A Report on Earnings and Long-Term Career Paths* (Washington, DC: Association of American Colleges and Universities, 2014), 9; David J. Deming and Kadeem Noray, "Earnings Dynamics, Changing Job Skills, and STEM Careers,"

Quarterly Journal of Economics 135, no. 4 (2020): 1965–2005; Fiorina, *Tough Choices*, 10–11; Fiorina, "Commencement Address."

20. Kristen Broady and Brad Hershbein, "Major Decisions: What Graduates Earn over Their Lifetimes," Brookings Institution, October 8, 2020, https:// www.brookings.edu/articles/major-decisions-what-graduates-earn-over -their-lifetimes/; The Hamilton Project, "Career Earnings by College Major," October 8, 2020, https://www.hamiltonproject.org/data/career-earnings-by -college-major/; George Anders, *You Can Do Anything: The Surprising Power of a "Useless" Liberal Arts Education* (New York: Back Bay Books, 2019), 152–56; Lisa Rogak, *Rachel Maddow: A Biography* (New York: Thomas Dunne Books, 2020), 31; Joe Pompeo, "Exclusive: Rachel Maddow Gives Her First Interview as She Steps Back from the Nightly Grind and Revs Up for Her Next Act," *Vanity Fair*, August 7, 2022, https://www.vanityfair.com/news/2022/08/exclusive -rachel-maddow-gives-her-first-interview-as-she-steps-back.

21. France Córdova, "Commencement Address," Stanford University, June 11, 2022, https://news.stanford.edu/2022/06/11/commencement-address-class -2020-france-cordova/; Reed Hastings, "Commencement Address," Stanford University, June 12, 2022, https://news.stanford.edu/2022/06/12/commencement -address-class-2022-reed-hastings/.

Reflection—What to study. Damon, *Path to Purpose*, 145.

22. Tina Seelig, *What I Wish I Knew When I Was 20: A Crash Course on Making Your Place in the World* (New York: HarperOne, 2019), 69, 71; Atul Gawande, *The Checklist Manifesto: How to Get Things Right* (New York: Picador, 2010), 48; Atul Gawande, *Complications: A Surgeon's Notes on an Imperfect Science* (New York: Picador, 2002), 58, 105.

23. Carol Dweck, *Mindset: Changing the Way You Think to Fulfil Your Potential* (London: Robinson, 2017), 6, 7, 258; Jo Boaler, *Limitless Mind: Learn, Lead, and Live without Barriers* (New York: HarperOne, 2019), 11, 13, 40, 50.

24. Tom Kelley and David Kelley, *Creative Confidence: Unleashing the Creative Potential within Us All* (New York: Crown Business, 2013), 69–70; Kristin Toussaint, "Premature Births Have Tripled in Ukraine. This Nonprofit Is Donating Portable Incubators," *Fast Company*, May 5, 2022, https://www .fastcompany.com/90750093/premature-births-have-tripled-in-ukraine-this -nonprofit-is-donating-portable-incubators; Myra Strober, *Sharing the Work: What My Family and Career Taught Me about Breaking Through (and Holding the Door Open for Others)* (Cambridge, MA: MIT Press, 2017), 12, 75, 213.

25. Dianne Feinstein, "Commencement Address," Stanford University, June 13, 1993, https://awpc.cattcenter.iastate.edu/2017/03/21/commencement -address-at-stanford-university-june-13-1993/; Linda Heuman, "The Best Medicine: Atul Gawande Works to Learn How Good Doctors Improve," *Stanford Magazine*, July/August 2007, https://stanfordmag.org/contents/the-best -medicine; Markoff, *Whole Earth*, 26; Albert M. Camarillo, *Compton in My Soul: A Life in Pursuit of Racial Equality* (Stanford: Stanford University Press, 2024), 121; Charles Schwab, *Invested: Changing Forever the Way Americans Invest* (New

York: Currency, 2019), 26–27; Charles Schwab, "Charles Schwab Corporation Investor Relations," About Schwab, accessed August 21, 2024, https://www.aboutschwab.com/investor-relations.

26. Kelley and Kelley, *Creative Confidence*, 112, 114, 146; Richard Engel, "Commencement Address," Stanford University, June 14, 2015, https://news.stanford.edu/2015/06/14/engel-commence-text-061415/; Richard Engel, *And Then All Hell Broke Loose: Two Decades in the Middle East* (New York: Simon & Schuster, 2016), 6, 150, 184.

27. Richard C. Levin, *The Worth of the University* (New Haven: Yale University Press, 2013), 4, 64; Richard C. Levin, *The Work of the University* (New Haven: Yale University Press, 2003), 73; Ken Bain, *What the Best College Students Do* (Cambridge, MA: Harvard University Press, 2012), 218–19.

28. Sarah Stein Greenberg, *Creative Acts for Curious People: How to Think, Create, and Lead in Unconventional Ways* (New York: Ten Speed Press, 2021), 212–13; Majo Molfino, *Break the Good Girl Myth: How to Dismantle Outdated Rules, Unleash Your Power, and Design a More Purposeful Life* (New York: HarperOne, 2021), 76–77.

29. Rogak, *Rachel Maddow*, 31; Michael McFaul, *From Cold War to Hot Peace: An American Ambassador in Putin's Russia* (Boston: Houghton Mifflin Harcourt, 2018), 2–3.

30. Derek Bok, *Our Underachieving Colleges: A Candid Look at How Much Students Learn and Why They Should Be Learning More* (Princeton: Princeton University Press, 2008), 68, 113; Levin, *Worth of the University*, 89–90; Levin, *Work of the University*, 82.

31. Stephen L. Carter, *Civility: Manners, Morals, and the Etiquette of Democracy* (New York: Harper Perennial, 1999), 139–40; Stephen L. Carter, *Integrity* (New York: Harper Perennial, 1997), 222; Chip Heath and Dan Heath, *Decisive: How to Make Better Choices in Life and Work* (New York: Currency, 2013), 99, 100.

32. Peter Thiel with Blake Masters, *Zero to One: Notes on Startups, or How to Build the Future* (New York: Currency, 2014), 9, 10–11; Reid Hoffman, June Cohen, and Deron Triff, *Masters of Scale: Surprising Truths from the World's Most Successful Entrepreneurs* (New York: Currency, 2021), 8, 60, 217.

33. William F. Woo, *Letters from the Editor: Lessons on Journalism and Life* (Columbia: University of Missouri Press, 2007), 92, 139, 178; Jim Tankersley, *The Riches of This Land: The Untold, True Story of America's Middle Class* (New York: Public Affairs, 2020), 237.

34. Knight, *Shoe Dog*, 9–10, 29; Rae, "Commencement Address"; Issa Rae, *The Misadventures of Awkward Black Girl* (New York: Atria, 2016), 47.

35. Booker, *United*, 23, 26, 27; Personal communication, August 4, 2023.

36. Reid Hoffman and Ben Casnocha, *The Start-Up of You: Adapt to the Future, Invest in Yourself, and Transform Your Career* (New York: Crown Business, 2012), 23, 39–40, 68; Dan Edelstein, "Mind over Major: The Case for Using College to Become More Interesting," *Stanford Magazine*, September 2022, https://stanfordmag.org/contents/mind-over-major.

37. Nicholas Carlson, *Marissa Mayer and the Fight to Save Yahoo!* (New York: Twelve, 2015), 140, 143; Hastings, "Commencement Address."

38. Julian Castro, *An Unlikely Journey: Waking Up from My American Dream* (New York: Little Brown, 2018), 110; Condoleezza Rice, *Extraordinary, Ordinary People: A Memoir of Family* (New York: Three Rivers Press, 2010), 192, 289.

39. Personal communication, August 16, 2023; Personal communication, August 4, 2023.

40. Seppala, *Happiness Track*, 5, 11–12, 17; Jenny Odell, *How to Do Nothing: Resisting the Attention Economy* (Brooklyn, NY: Melville House, 2019), 87, 89, 185.

41. hooks, *Wounds of Passion*, 25; bell hooks, *Teaching Community: A Pedagogy of Hope* (New York, Routledge, 2003), 42; Rogak, *Rachel Maddow*, 179.

42. Seelig, *What I Wish I Knew*, 163–64, 179; Brown, "Commencement Address."

43. Szu-Chi Huang and Jennifer Aaker, "It's the Journey, Not the Destination: How Metaphor Drives Growth after Goal Attainment," *Journal of Personality and Social Psychology* 117, no. 4 (2019): 697–720; Deborah Liu, *Take Back Your Power: 10 New Rules for Women at Work* (Grand Rapids, MI: Zondervan Books, 2022), 45–46, 183.

44. Walter Mischel, *The Marshmallow Test: Why Self-Control Is the Engine of Success* (New York: Little, Brown Spark, 2015), 3, 67; B. J. Fogg, *Tiny Habits: The Small Changes That Change Everything* (Boston, Mariner Books, 2020), 2, 5, 296.

45. Simone Stolzoff, *The Good Enough Job: Reclaiming Life from Work* (New York: Portfolio, 2023), 76–77, 139; Nir Eyal with Julie Li, *Indistractable: How to Control Your Attention and Choose Your Life* (Dallas, TX: BenBella, 2019), 57, 71.

46. Mae Jemison, "Commencement Address," Stanford University, June 16, 1996, https://web.archive.org/web/20151009101545/https://web.stanford .edu/dept/spec_coll/uarch/commencement/SC1020_1996.pdf; Zimbardo and Boyd, *Time Paradox*, 110, 302–3, 318.

47. Heath and Heath, *Decisive*, 188; Odell, *How to Do Nothing*, xviii, 15, 179.

48. Seppala, *Happiness Track*, 64, 113, 122; Kelly McGonigal, *The Joy of Movement: How Exercise Helps Us Find Happiness, Hope, Connection, and Courage* (New York: Penguin Random House, 2019), 2, 213.

49. Personal communication, July 28, 2023; Personal communication, August 4, 2023.

50. Emma Coleman, "Baccalaureate Speech," Stanford University, June 17, 2017, https://news.stanford.edu/2017/06/17/prepared-text-student-emma -colemans-baccalaureate-speech/; Bobby Pragada, "Anecdotes from My Sports Life," *Stanford Daily*, June 16, 2019.

51. Lauren Fleshman, *Good for a Girl: A Woman Running in a Man's World* (New York: Penguin Press, 2023), 69, 73; Carrie Holmes, *Happier Hour: How to Beat Distraction, Expand Your Time, and Focus on What Matters Most* (New York: Gallery Books, 2022), 113, 240.

52. Susan Rice, *Tough Love: My Story of the Things Worth Fighting For* (New York: Simon & Schuster, 2020), 98, 100; Rae Jemison, *Find Where the*

Wind Goes: Moments from My Life (Houston, TX: Signal Hill Road Publishing, 2020), 125–26.

53. Personal communication, July 28, 2023; Personal communication, August 5, 2023.

54. Rae, "Commencement Address"; Samantha Wong, "Sincerely, Me," *Stanford Daily*, June 18, 2018, https://stanforddaily.com/2018/06/18/wong -sincerely-me/.

55. Kawasaki, *Wise Guy*, 22, 54, 56–57; Rice, *Tough Love*, 104; McFaul, *Cold War*, 76.

56. Mark S. Granovetter, "The Strength of Weak Ties," *American Journal of Sociology* 78, no. 6 (1973): 1360–80; Stanford News, "The Real Strength of Weak Ties," September 15, 2022, https://news.stanford.edu/2022/09/15/ real-strength-weak-ties/; Randall Stross, *A Practical Education: Why Liberal Arts Majors Make Great Employees* (Stanford: Stanford University Press, 2017), 154, 157.

57. Erin Woo, "Letter from the Editor: An Editor's Farewell," *Stanford Daily*, June 3, 2021, https://stanforddaily.com/2021/06/03/letter-from-the-editor-an -editors-farewell/; Hannah Knowles, "One Last Pitch," *Stanford Daily*, June 16, 2019, https://stanforddaily.com/2019/06/16/knowles-one-last-pitch/.

58. Cory Booker, "Commencement Address," Stanford University, June 17, 2012, https://news.stanford.edu/2012/06/17/transcript-newark-n-j-mayor -cory-bookers-remarks-stanfords-commencement-2012/; Olatunde Sobom-ehin and Sam Seidel, *Creative Hustle: Blaze Your Own Path and Make Work That Matters* (New York: Ten Speed Press, 2022), 63.

59. Amanda Rizkalla, "FLI Abroad," *Stanford Daily*, November 20, 2019, https://stanforddaily.com/2019/11/20/fli-abroad/; Engel, "Commencement Address."

60. Personal communication, April 9, 2016; Tankersley, *Riches of This Land*, 252–53.

61. Hakeem Oluseyi and Joshua Horwitz, *A Quantum Life: My Unlikely Jour-ney from the Street to the Stars* (New York: Ballantine Books, 2021), 285–86; Emma Master, "A Pathway to Progress," *Stanford Daily*, April 21, 2022, https:// stanforddaily.com/2022/04/21/from-the-community-a-pathway-to-progress/; From the Community, "'Are You Going to CAPS?,'" *Stanford Daily*, February 25, 2019.

62. Lenora Chu, *Little Soldiers: An American Boy, a Chinese School, and the Global Race to Achieve* (New York: HarperCollins, 2017), 35; Jesmyn Ward, *Men We Reaped: A Memoir* (New York: Bloomsbury, 2014), 22, 195; MacArthur Foun-dation, "MacArthur Fellows Program: Jesmyn Ward," October 11, 2017, https:// www.macfound.org/fellows/class-of-2017/jesmyn-ward#searchresults.

63. Atul Gawande, *Better: A Surgeon's Notes on Performance* (New York: Picador, 2007), 251–52; Personal communication, August 3, 2023.

64. Tankersley, *Riches of This Land*, 10, 95; Molly McCully Brown, *Places I've Taken My Body* (New York: Persea Books, 2020), 88, 90.

65. Claude M. Steele, *Whistling Vivaldi: How Stereotypes Affect Us and What We Can Do* (New York: Norton, 2010), 167; Kory Gaines, "Bodies of Genius,"

Stanford Office for Religious & Spiritual Life, https://orsl.stanford.edu/meeting -moment/monthly-reflections.

66. Stephen Murphy-Shigematsu, *When Half Is Whole: Multiethnic Asian American Identities* (Stanford: Stanford University Press, 2012), 219–20; Vicki L. Ruiz, *From Out of the Shadows: Mexican Women in Twentieth-Century America* (New York: Oxford University Press, 2008), xi, xiii.

67. Chu, *Little Soldiers*, 43, 290–92; Lily Zheng and Inge Hansen, *The Ethical Sellout: Maintaining Your Integrity in the Age of Compromise* (Oakland, CA: Berrett-Koehler Publishers, 2019), 8, 149, 167.

68. Personal communication, October 19, 2023.

69. Rice, *Extraordinary*, 157–58; Rae, *Misadventures*, 159–60, 162–63.

70. Fleshman, *Good for a Girl*, 156, 159; Seema Yasmin, *Muslim Women Are Everything: Stereotype-Shattering Stories of Courage, Inspiration, and Adventure* (New York: Harper Design, 2020), 2–3, 21.

71. Paula M. Moya, *The Social Imperative: Race, Close Reading, and Contemporary Literary Criticism* (Stanford: Stanford University Press, 2016), 54, 58, 165; Waka T. Brown, *While I Was Away* (New York: Quill Tree Books, 2021), 291, 301.

72. Steele, *Whistling Vivaldi*, 3–4, 166; Ward, *Men We Reaped*, 202–3; Jesmyn Ward, *Navigate Your Stars* (New York: Scribner, 2020), n.p.

73. Lynn Sherr, *Sally Ride: America's First Woman in Space* (New York: Simon & Schuster, 2015), 289, 314, 316; Barres, *Autobiography*, 56–57, 114.

74. Jemison, *Find Where*, 140–41, 147; Stephen L. Carter, *Reflections of an Affirmative Action Baby* (New York: Basic Books, 1991), 1–2, 4, 6.

75. Liu, *Take Back Your Power*, 31, 123; Personal communication, September 20, 2023.

76. Jennifer L. Eberhardt, *Biased: Uncovering the Hidden Prejudice That Shapes What We See, Think, and Do* (New York: Viking, 2019), 100, 112; Brian Lowery, *Selfless: The Social Creation of "You"* (New York: HarperCollins, 2023), 83–84.

77. Darnell Carson, "Tomorrow Never Comes, but We Chase It Anyway," Stanford Office for Religious & Spiritual Life, https://orsl.stanford.edu/ meeting-moment/monthly-reflections; Oluseyi and Horwitz, *Quantum Life*, 199, 215, 234.

Reflection—Be yourself. Steele, *Whistling Vivaldi*, 167.

78. Stephen Breyer, "Commencement Address," Stanford University, June 15, 1997, https://www.c-span.org/video/?87293-1/stanford-university -commencement; Anthony M. Kennedy, *The US Supreme Court Decision on Marriage Equality, as Delivered by Justice Anthony Kennedy* (Brooklyn, NY: Melville House, 2015), 21, 26; Anthony Kennedy, "Commencement Address," Stanford University, June 14, 2009, https://news.stanford.edu/2009/06/14/ text-justice-kennedys-2009-commencement-address/.

79. Barry Fischer, "Baccalaureate Speech," Stanford University, June 14, 2008, https://news.stanford.edu/2008/06/14/speech-fischer-likens-life-giant

-jigsaw-puzzle/; Paul Rogat Loeb, *Soul of a Citizen: Living with Conviction in Challenging Times* (New York: St. Martin's Griffin, 2010), 11, 21, 355.

80. Adam Schiff, *Midnight in Washington: How We Almost Lost Our Democracy and Still Could* (New York: Random House, 2021), 29; LaDoris Hazzard Cordell, *Her Honor: My Life on the Bench . . . What Works, What's Broken, and How to Change It* (New York: Celadon Books, 2021), 267, 294.

81. Eamonn Callan, "Re: The Thought Police: On College Campuses, How Do We Achieve Both Civility and Candor?," *Stanford Magazine*, September 2017, https://stanfordmag.org/contents/re-the-thought-police; Carter, *Reflections*, 183–85.

82. Tess Winston, "With Some of My Fellow Stanford Law Students, There's No Room for Agreement," *Washington Post*, April 3, 2023, https://www.washingtonpost.com/opinions/2023/04/03/stanford-law-school-intimidation-of-moderates/; Shanto Iyengar, Yphtach Lelkes, Matthew Levendusky, Neil Malhotra, and Sean J. Westwood, "The Origins and Consequences of Affective Polarization in the United States," *Annual Review of Political Science* 22 (2019): 129–46; Matthew Tyler and Shanto Iyengar, "Learning to Dislike Your Opponents: Political Socialization in the Era of Polarization," *American Political Science Review* 117, no. 1 (2023): 347–54.

83. Ted Koppel, "Commencement Address," Stanford University, June 14, 1998, https://www.101bananas.com/library2/koppel.html; Carter, *Civility*, 18; Carter, *Integrity*, 223.

84. Courtney Cooperman, "Senior Column: Reflections from the Castle," *Stanford Daily*, June 13, 2020, https://stanforddaily.com/2020/06/13/reflections-from-the-castle/; Michael Wines, "Dissecting Romney's Vietnam Stance at Stanford," *New York Times*, September 11, 2012, https://www.nytimes.com/2012/09/12/us/politics/at-stanford-romney-stood-ground-on-vietnam.html; Margot Mifflin, "Obama at Occidental," *New Yorker*, October 3, 2012, https://www.newyorker.com/news/news-desk/obama-at-occidental#slide_ss_0=1; Rice, *Tough Love*, 105.

85. Martin Luther King Jr., "Remaining Awake through a Great Revolution," National Cathedral, Washington, DC, March 31, 1968, https://www.seemeonline.com/history/mlk-jr-awake.htm; Melissa De Witte, "Active Listening, Learning Are Some of the Skills to Help Democracy Thrive, Say Experts at COLLEGE Roundtable Event," *Stanford Report*, January 18, 2023, https://news.stanford.edu/report/2023/01/18/democracy-starts-listening-one-another/; Pamela S. Karlan, "Remarks in Recognition of Women's History Month," Washington, DC, March 30, 2021, https://www.justice.gov/opa/speech/pamela-s-karlan-principal-deputy-attorney-general-civil-rights-division-delivers-remarks; George P. Shultz, *Learning from Experience* (Stanford: Hoover Institution Press, 2016), 36.

86. Eyal, *Indistractable*, 3; Fronsdal, *Issue at Hand*, 6, 17, 111.

87. Stolzoff, *Good Enough Job*, 196–97; John McEnroe, "Commencement Address," Stanford University, June 18, 2023, https://news.stanford.edu/report/2023/06/18/2023-commencement-address-john-mcenroe/.

88. Terry Castle, "Don't Pick Up: Why Kids Need to Separate from Their Parents," *Chronicle of Higher Education*, May 6, 2012, https://www.chronicle.com/article/dont-pick-up/; Jonathan Levin, "Dean's Remarks," Stanford University, June 17, 2023, https://www.gsb.stanford.edu/experience/news-history/commencement/dean-remarks.

89. Ward, *Navigate Your Stars*, n.p.; Hennessy, *Leading Matters*, 31–32, 136, 140.

90. Michael Tubbs, *The Deeper the Roots: A Memoir of Hope and Home* (New York: Flatiron Books, 2021), 3, 50; Mark Applebaum, "The Value of Accountability: An Open Letter to My Students," Stanford Canvas, March 2023.

91. Dana Gioia, "Commencement Address," Stanford University, June 17, 2007, https://news.stanford.edu/2007/06/17/gioia-graduates-trade-easy-pleasures-complex-challenging-ones/; Personal communication, May 9, 2023.

92. David Marchese, "What If Instead of Trying to Manage Your Time, You Set It Free?," *New York Times*, May 14, 2023, https://www.nytimes.com/interactive/2023/05/15/magazine/jenny-odell-interview.html; Brown, "Commencement Address."

93. Edward Slingerland, *Trying Not to Try: Ancient China, Modern Science, and the Power of Spontaneity* (New York: Broadway Books, 2014), 203, 212; McGonigal, *Joy of Movement*, 2, 166, 214.

94. McEnroe, "Commencement Address"; Gretchen Carlson, *Getting Real* (New York: Viking, 2015), 63, 73, 251.

95. Elissa Epel, *The Stress Prescription: Seven Days to More Joy and Ease* (New York: Penguin Life, 2022), 18–19, 24–25; Grace Carroll, "Against Ambition," *Stanford Daily*, June 13, 2024, https://stanforddaily.com/2024/06/13/against-ambition/.

96. Louis E. Newman, *Thinking Critically in College: The Essential Handbook for Student Success* (New York: Radius Book Group, 2023), 40, 46–47, 61; Ashish Goel, *Drawing on Courage: Risks Worth Taking and Stands Worth Making* (New York: Ten Speed Press, 2022), 26.

97. Seppala, *Happiness Track*, 5; Loeb, *Soul of a Citizen*, 11–12.

98. Alejandro Salinas, "Thank You, Stanford," *Stanford Daily*, June 12, 2021, https://stanforddaily.com/2021/06/12/salinas-thank-you-stanford/; Jennifer Aaker and Naomi Bagdonas, *Humor, Seriously: Why Humor Is a Secret Weapon in Business and Life (and How Anyone Can Harness It. Even You)* (New York: Currency, 2021), 65, 224, 226.

99. Julian Castro, "Democratic National Convention Keynote Address," Charlotte, NC, September 4, 2012, https://www.npr.org/2012/09/04/160574895/transcript-julian-castros-dnc-keynote-address; Castro, *Unlikely Journey*, 40; Booker, *United*, 11, 21; Booker, "Commencement Address."

100. Roth, *Achievement Habit*, 112, 121; Patricia Ryan Madson, *Improv Wisdom: Don't Prepare, Just Show Up* (New York: Bell Tower, 2005), 27, 35, 38, 53.

ABOUT THE AUTHOR
AND ILLUSTRATOR

JAMES T. ("JAY") HAMILTON is Vice Provost for Undergraduate Education and Hearst Professor of Communication at Stanford University. The winner of eight teaching awards at Harvard, Duke, and Stanford, he's spent decades teaching and mentoring undergraduates and designing programs to help them thrive in college.

As chair of the First-Year Requirement Governance Board at Stanford, Hamilton helped implement the Civic, Liberal, and Global Education requirement for first-year students. This set of classes prompts students to reflect on the goals of their college education and their roles as citizens in the twenty-first century.

Hamilton is the author of three award-winning books about media research. He earned a BA in economics and government (summa cum laude) and a PhD in economics from Harvard University.

JIM TOOMEY is an internationally published humor writer and syndicated cartoonist best known as the creator of the popular comic strip *Sherman's Lagoon*, published daily in over 150 newspapers, including *The Washington Post*, the *San Francisco Chronicle*, and the *Chicago Tribune*.